Anatomy
of the
Ship

The Armed Transport

BOUNTY

**Anatomy
of the
Ship**

The Armed Transport
BOUNTY

John McKay

CONWAY
MARITIME PRESS

ACKNOWLEDGEMENTS

It is with sincere gratitude that I thank the following individuals and institutions for their assistance with this project: Arthur Christian (HMS *Bounty* Society International), Ron Coleman (Queensland Museum), A G Credland (Hull Town Docks Museum), Environment Canada – Parks and Fort Langley National Historic Park, John Harland, Leonard McCann (Vancouver Maritime Museum), E J Russell (The Hull Trinity House), and my wife Ellen.

Frontispiece
1. The full-size replica of *Bounty* built for the 1962 film *Mutiny on the Bounty*, seen here in Calais Harbour during the same year. *John Mannering*

© John McKay 1989

First published in Great Britain 1989 by
Conway Maritime Press Limited
24 Bride Lane, Fleet Street
London EC4Y 8DR

British Library Cataloguing in Publication Data

McKay, John
  The armed transport Bounty.
  1. Great Britain. Merchant sailing ships.
  Design & construction
  I. Title
  623.8′224′0941

  ISBN 0 85177 502 0

Designed by Jonathan Doney
Typeset by Inforum Typesetting, Portsmouth
Printed by The Bath Press, Bath

Contents

Introduction   6
Ship's history   6
Career summary   7
Hull construction   7
Refit   8
Decoration   9
Steering gear   10
Ground tackle   10
Pumps   11
Boats   11
Crew and accommodation   12
Masts and yards   12
Sails   13
Rigging   14
Ordnance   14

The Photographs   15

The Drawings   22
A.   General arrangement and lines   23
B.   Hull construction   35
C.   External hull   49
D.   Internal hull   56
E.   Fittings   77
F.   Armament   83
G.   Masts and spars   84
H.   Rigging   96
I.   Sails   113
J.   Boats   119

Introduction

SHIP'S HISTORY

In 1775, The Standing Committee of West India Planters and Merchants decided that it would be to their advantage to introduce bread-fruit trees and mangosteen into the West India colonies as an inexpensive source of food for their plantation slaves. A prize was offered to anyone who successfully transported bread-fruit trees from the East Indies to the West Indies and, in 1777, a fund was set up to encourage interest in this project. Despite these initiatives ten years lapsed before any further action was taken. In May, 1787, however, the Admiralty was approached by one of the Principal Secretaries of State, Lord Sydney, who, in a letter, outlined His Majesty's interest in this mission. Obviously private enterprise was not interested, so the Government and the Royal Navy became involved.

At this time it was common practice for the Navy to buy or lease ships for a specific purpose, so on 9 May 1787 the Admiralty ordered the immediate purchase by the Navy Board of a suitable vessel, not exceeding 250 tons burthen. Five ships, plus one latecomer, *Harriot*, were considered by the Board:

Lynx, 300 tons, Mr Campbell, lying at Greenland Dock, £2200;
Shepherdess, 270 tons, Messrs Wellbank, Sharp and Brown, lying at Pickle Herring Chain, £2050;
Bethia, 230 tons, Messrs Wellbank, Sharp and Brown, lying at Old Wapping Stairs, £2600;
William Pitt, 240 tons, Mr Dawson, lying at King Edward Stairs, £1200;
New ship, 240 or 250 tons, Mr Elches, at Newcastle, £9 10s 0d per ton.

The Navy Board reported to the Admiralty that they intended to purchase *Bethia*, and the Admiralty appointed Sir Joseph Banks, an eminent botanist who had sailed with Captain Cook, to examine her and to supervise her fitting out. The Board also ordered the officers of Deptford Yard to survey *Bethia*, and on 23 May Deptford submitted dimensions and value estimate to the Board:

Length of the Keel for Tonnage	69ft 11⅜in
Breadth Extream	24ft 4in
Depth in Hold	11ft 4in
Burthen in Tons	220 ²⁶/₉₄
Length of the lower deck	85ft 1½in
Beams 12 in No. Square	1ft 0in

Height between decks Afore		6ft 3in
Midsh		5ft 7in
Abaft		7ft 0in
Upper deck		91ft 0in
Do. flush fore and aft depth of waste [waist]		0ft 4½in
Main Hatch Fore and Aft		9ft 1in
Main Hatch Thwartship		6ft 1in
Great Cabbin		11ft 0in
Steerage		12ft 0in

	£	s	d
Value of the Hull, Masts and Yards	1718	0	0
Anchors	64	15	0
Add 2½ per cent. Discount on £1782 15s 0d	37	17	0
Total	1820	12	8

Bethia was bought on 26 May and her cost estimate must have been adjusted upward, as her final purchase price, according to Admiralty records, was £1950. It is interesting to compare this figure with the asking price of £2600.

Apart from the above, little is known about *Bethia*, as ships of her size and character were very common at the time (Britain had the largest national fleet of merchant ships) and details were therefore not recorded. We do know however that she was built in the No 2 dry dock on the River Hull, that her keel was probably laid in 1783, and that as she was a relatively flat-bottomed merchantman, 'roomy in accommodation and stowage'. This flat-bottomed hull shape was an important feature when considering *Bounty*'s mission; not only was hold capacity critical (*Bounty* was provisioned for 18 months), but also a flat-bottomed ship ran less risk of falling over if by chance she grounded on one of the many reefs in the South Seas. Indeed, *Bounty* did run aground at Tahiti, as Bligh notes; 'but to our great surprise, we found that the ship was aground forwards. She had run on so easy, that we had not perceived it at the time'. Bligh also notes that she was 'an excellent sea boat'.

On 26 May 1787 *Bethia* was moved from Wapping Old Stairs to Deptford Yard to begin fitting out for her intended voyage to the South Seas; Sir Joseph Banks arrived on 8 June. Also on 8 June, the Admiralty instructed the Navy Board to have *Bethia* registered on the Royal Navy Ships List as HM Armed Vessel *Bounty*, and here is an interesting point: although *Bounty* was fully rigged as a ship she was not large enough to require a Post Captain in command; as her Scheme of Complement called for a Lieutenant to command (although he was termed Captain in his role as ship's commander) *Bounty* was classified as an 'Armed Vessel'.

Bligh was appointed to *Bounty* on 16 August, and on that date he became involved in supervising her fitting out. On 3 September the ship was taken out of dock and brought alongside the hulk, where her masts were taken out and shortened, although Bligh notes that 'the carpenters and joiners remained on board, as they had a great deal of work to finish'. By 9 October *Bounty* was at Long Reach, where provisioning was completed, and on the 15th Bligh received orders to proceed to Spithead. Owing to bad weather, the ship did not arrive there until 4 November. Lord Hood, commander at Spithead, gave Bligh his final orders on 24 November but, again due to the weather, *Bounty* was not able to sail until 23 December, which she did 'with a fair wind'.

Bounty arrived at Tenerife (Canary Islands) on 4 January 1788 and after six days of provisioning sailed for Cape Horn. After attempting to round the Horn for thirty days Bligh was forced to abandon this course, and on 22 April bore away for the Cape of Good Hope. *Bounty* anchored at False Bay (South Africa) on 24 May. Some provisioning and repair work was carried out at False Bay and she put to sea again on 29 June, arriving at Adventure Bay (Van Diemen's Land) on 20 August for a stay of fifteen days. On 4 September *Bounty* left Van Diemen's Land and on 25 October she was within sight of the island of Matea, arriving at Tahiti the following day. Her passage from Spithead to Tahiti had taken slightly more than ten months.

On 4 April 1789 *Bounty* departed Tahiti after a stay of over five months. From 5 April to 27 April she made stops at several small islands while sailing westward towards Endeavour Strait; on the morning of the 28 April, while the ship lay off Torfua, part of her crew mutinied under the leadership of Fletcher Christian, took command of the ship, and put Bligh and eighteen loyal followers into the 23-foot launch.

From this point *Bounty*'s history is not easily followed as we do not have Bligh's meticulous log to go by. We do know, however, that Christian first took her to the island of Tubai, where he was forced away by the natives, and then back to Tahiti. Christian tried again to approach Tubai and was driven off a second time, after which *Bounty* again returned to Tahiti. With a reduced crew of mutineers, supplemented by Tahitians, Christian finally found refuge at Pitcairn Island, where *Bounty* anchored in the bay that is named after her. Early in 1790 the ship was beached, stripped and burned to the waterline, and what remains of her still lies at the bottom of Bounty Bay.

CAREER SUMMARY

1783: Probable year that *Bethia*'s keel was laid

5 May 1787: Lord Sydney writes to the Admiralty informing them of His Majesty's desire to promote the interests of the West India Planters and Merchants

9 May 1787: Admiralty receives Lord Sydney's letter and instructs the Navy Board to purchase a suitable vessel for a South Seas mission

10 May 1787: Navy Board advertises for a ship

16 May 1787: Navy Board considers the purchase of one of five ships with one latecomer

17 May 1787: Navy Board reports to the Admiralty that they intend to buy *Bethia*

21 May 1787: Admiralty informs the Navy Board that Sir Joseph Banks is to view *Bethia*

23 May 1787: Deptford Yard submits its report on *Bethia* to the Navy Board

26 May 1787: *Bethia* purchased and moved to Deptford Yard

31 May 1787: Admiralty gives directions to the Navy Board concerning *Bethia*'s fitting out

6 June 1787: Deptford reports to the Navy Board regarding guns, masts and yards

8 June 1787: Sir Joseph Banks attends *Bethia*; the Admiralty instructs the Navy Board to have *Bounty* registered on the list of Royal Navy Ships; the Navy Board specifies changes that are to be made to *Bounty*'s masts and yards

20 June 1787: Deptford officers report to Navy Board concerning *Bounty*'s boat requirements

25 June 1787: Deptford Yard sends draughts of *Bounty* showing proposed changes to the Navy Board

6 July 1787: Navy Board returns altered draughts to Deptford Yard

14 August 1787: *Bounty* undocked

16 August 1787: Admiralty appoints Lieutenant William Bligh to command *Bounty*, and orders the Navy Board to have her manned with a crew of forty-five and victualled for twelve months (Bligh states that *Bounty* was 'stored and victualled for eighteen months')

30 August 1787: Admiralty directs the Navy Board to have *Bounty*'s masts and yards cut down in accordance with Bligh's request

3 September 1787: *Bounty* brought alongisde the masting hulk

4 September 1787: masts unstepped and cut down

9 October 1787: *Bounty* moved to Long Reach

15 October 1787: ordered to Spithead

4 November 1787: arrives at Spithead

24 November 1787: Lord Hood orders *Bounty* to sail

23 December 1787: *Bounty* sails from Spithead

24 December 1787 – 3 January 1788: Passage to Tenerife

4 January – 10 January 1788: provisioning at Tenerife

11 January – 22 March 1788: passage to Cape Horn

23 March – 21 April 1788: *Bounty* tries unsuccessfully to round Cape Horn

22 April – 23 May 1788: passage to Cape of Good Hope

24 May – 28 June 1788: provisioning and repair work at False Bay

29 June – 19 August 1788: passage to Adventure Bay

20 August – 3 September 1788: provisioning at Adventure Bay

4 September – 25 October 1788: passage to Tahiti

26 October 1788: *Bounty* anchors at Matavai Bay, Tahiti

27 October 1788 – 3 April 1789: at Tahiti

4 April 1789: *Bounty* leaves Tahiti

5 April – 27 April 1789: *Bounty* sails westward towards Endeavour Strait

28 April 1789: Fletcher Christian leads a successful mutiny against Bligh and takes command of *Bounty*

May – September 1789: Christian, in command of *Bounty*, searches for refuge in the South Seas

23 January 1790: *Bounty* run aground at Pitcairn Island; she is stripped and burned

HULL CONSTRUCTION

The drawings of *Bounty*'s hull in this book are based on two sets of contemporary draughts; the first was prepared to illustrate *Bethia* for the Admiralty, and the second, based on the first, to show proposed changes. The first draught is dated 25 June 1787 and shows *Bethia* as she was purchased; the second, dated 19 November 1787, embodies the modifications required by the Admiralty, and was used by Deptford Yard. Both sets of drawings show an outboard profile, half breadth plan and body plan on the first sheet and plans of the upper deck, lower deck and hold on the second sheet. As no major structural changes were made, the half breadth plans and body plans are identical on both sets. The drawings were prepared at a scale of ¼ inch to the foot (¹/₄₈ scale) and as paper is prone to shrinking and expanding it is fortunate that the draughtsman provided a linear scale to both outboard profiles.

Both draughts have an outline specification giving dimensions and tonnage, and here there is a contradiction. The specification dated 25 June reads:

Length of the Range of the Deck	85ft 1½in
Do. of the Keel for Tonnage	69ft 11³⁄₈in
Breadth Extreme	24ft 4in
Burthen in Tons	220 ²⁶⁄₉₄

The Specification dated 19 November reads:

Length of the Range of the Deck	84ft 6in
Do. Keel for Tonnage	69ft 9in
Breadth extreme	24ft 10in
Depth in Hold	11ft 4in
Burthen in Tons	228 ⁶⁴⁄₉₄

The difference between specifications is easily explained: just prior to acquiring *Bethia* the Deptford yard officers surveyed her and produced the early figures; they produced the second set after docking her and examining her more closely. It is therefore a safe assumption that the specification of 19 November is the more accurate, and indeed *Bounty*'s lower deck length (fore perpendicular to aft perpendicular) scales 84ft 6in. Her tonnage was calculated by the formula:

$$\frac{\text{length of keel} \times \text{breadth} \times \frac{1}{2} \text{breadth}}{94}$$

Bounty's draught shows a total of eleven station lines expressed as frame lines on the body plan. These are the Dead Flat, A to D forward and 1 to 6 aft. These lines were probably determined by the Deptford Yard surveyor, by taking internal measurements (to the outside of frames) and while they give enough information for a draughtsman to describe the ship's hull shape on paper, there are not enough of them for a shipwright to build a vessel. I arrived at *Bounty*'s framing plan by laying out the given station lines, from the draught, and assigning further lines at 4-foot intervals; these are the Dead Flat, (A) to O forward, and (3) to 24 aft. (The bracketed frame numbers occur amidships where all frames are identical to the frame at the Dead Flat). This system works perfectly if one allows that the surveyor took some measurements on the fore face of the frames and some measurements on the aft face, and that it was not essential that the frames he chose coincided with the original builder's lines. Based on 4-foot frame line intervals a room and space dimension of 12 inches is produced, the frames being 10 inches thick and spaced 2 inches apart. I have shown the original builder's lines circled on the half breadth plan and the framing plan.

As stated above, *Bounty*'s principal dimensions were given to the Navy Board on 23 May; these dimensions are very straightforward and the draught reflects them almost precisely. The sizes of the upper deck beams and hold platform beams can also be determined from the draughts, as well as details

of stem, keel and stern post and the size of the mast steps. From here on assumptions must be made based on ship-building practices of the day (see Table 1).

TABLE 1: DIMENSIONS OF BOUNTY'S FRAMING MEMBERS

Gunwale	3in × 12in
External plank	3in × 6in
Wale	5½in × 24in (3 strakes)
Strake above wale	4½in × 12in
Limber strake	4in × 10in
Keel	13in wide × 11in deep
Sole plate	2in
Keelson	13in wide × 14in deep
Ceiling	2½in thick
UPPER DECK	
Beams	8in to 12in wide × 5in to 8in deep (from draught)
Carlings	6in to 8in wide × 4in to 6in deep
Ledges	5in wide × 4in deep
Hanging and lodging knees	4in to 5in thick
Deck plank	2½in thick
Deck clamp	4in × 9in
LOWER DECK	
Beams	12in × 12in (from specification)
Carlings	8in wide × 7in deep
Ledges	6in wide × 5in deep
Hanging and lodging knees	5in to 8in thick
Deck plank	2½in thick
Deck clamp	4in × 10in
Waterway plank	5in × 4½in
Spirketting	3in thick (3 strakes)
Quickwork	2in thick

REFIT

One of the most fascinating aspects of *Bounty*, in terms of shipbuilding practices of the day, is that she was a merchant vessel not only converted into a 'floating greenhouse', but also refitted to meet the standards of the Royal Navy. Her refit took over three months to complete and cost more than her original purchase price. Refit and provisioning costs include £2504 spent on the hull, and £1952 spent on rigging and stores; with her purchase price of £1950 this gives a total of £6406.

The first alteration made was to sheath the ship with copper. When *Bethia* was acquired she was sheathed with wood to prevent sea worms from eating into her external planking. Although this was a very old practice it was not very successful; it involved coating the underwater area of a ship's hull with horse hair mixed in tar, then nailing planks over it. By 1778 it was standard policy to sheath all Navy vessels with copper and it is interesting to note that the merits of copper sheathing were first realized on ships returning from the South Seas. Coppering a ship's bottom was expensive, not so much for labour expended (a ship could be coppered surprisingly quickly), but because the cost of copper was high. The replacement of all iron hull fastenings by bronze, necessary because of the galvanic action between copper and iron, also added to the cost. To copper *Bounty* she would be beached broadside and careened over, her wood sheathing would then be removed, her iron fittings replaced with bronze ones, and she would then be sheathed with copper. She would then be refloated, turned around and the process would be repeated on the other side. After sheathing, a sole plate was stapled under her keel.

Bligh describes the conversion of *Bounty*'s lower deck into a garden in his account:

The between decks was divided in the following manner:- the great cabin was appropriated for the preservation of plants, and extended as far forward as the after hatchway. It had two large sky-lights, and on each side three scuttles for air, and was fitted with a false floor cut full of holes to contain the garden-pots, in which the plants were to be brought home. The deck was covered with lead, and at the foremost corners of the cabin were fixed pipes to carry off the water that had drained from the plants into tubs placed below to save it for future use. I had a small cabin on one side to sleep in, adjoining to the great cabin, and a place near the middle of the ship to eat in. The bulk-head of this apartment was at the after part of the main hatchway, and on each side of it were the berths of the mates and midshipmen; between these berths the arms-chest was placed. The cabin of the master, in which he always kept the key of the arms, was opposite to mine . . .

The cabin arrangement described by Bligh shows very clearly on the draught, and the Navy Board went into great detail in showing the pot racks. Provision was made for a total of 629 pots, of which 433 were 6 inches in diameter and 196 8 inches. Some work on the pot racks was done by *Bounty*'s crew, for on 15 November 1788 Bligh notes in the log, 'Carpenters still employed fixing additional stands for the plants in the cabin'. He also notes, 'Cooper making tubs and boxes' and that there were 774 pots, 39 tubs and 24 boxes.

Ventilation for the plants was considered to be important by the botanist, so two sets of gratings, which Bligh describes as 'sky-lights', were installed in the quarterdeck, one ahead of the mizzen mast and one aft of the wheel. To facilitate this addition a deck locker that sat just aft of the capstan was removed and carlings were added to support the coamings. The air scuttles referred to by Bligh were rectangular openings, roughly 5 inches by 12 inches, cut into the ship's side above the deck clamp. They were fitted with hinged lids which were caulked in poor weather and their location was governed by upper deck beams and lodging knees. The draught shows the foremost scuttle party behind a swivel stanchion.

Lining the cabin deck with lead, like copper sheathing, would have been expensive but was, however, necessary to conserve precious water. This, along with the other cabin changes, was done at the suggestion of Sir Joseph Banks. The berths for the Master's Mates and Midshipmen were merely canvas screens that hung from the deck above and as such do not appear on the draught. Further changes to *Bounty*'s lower deck involved reducing the size of the after companionway and installing a companionway forward, and removal of a Carpenter's and a Boatswain's cabin. A new Brodie stove was ordered and this was placed where the carpenter's cabin had stood. Support for the stove in the form of carlings would have been added in the lower deck and an opening for its chimney was cut and framed in the upper deck.

In addition to the gratings in the quarterdeck, changes were also made to *Bounty*'s upper deck. The Admiralty had determined that the ship was to carry four 4-pounder guns and ten half-pounder swivels. To accommodate the carriage guns, ports were cut and framed in the bulwarks, the deck framing was almost certainly strengthened with added carlings, and rings were installed for gun tackles. For the swivels, five stanchions were placed on either side of the ship. On the forecastle, two small air scuttles were cut into the deck and the belfry was changed; *Bethia*'s belfry consisted of two posts supporting an arched capital and cross bar, from which the bell hung. This fitting was removed and the bell was rehung on a metal hoop mounted on the windlass post. Aft, and here the draughts are somewhat ambiguous, it would seem that

small round ports were cut into the companionway and main hatch coamings. Also on the coamings, boat chocks were placed on the aft sides of the fore companionway and main hatch. *Bethia*'s boat was probably carried on her spare spars which were themselves carried on a crutch mounted above the fore brace bitts aft and over the windlass forward. To make room for *Bounty*'s boats the spars were carried on the channels and the crutch was removed. The bitts were made slightly smaller and strengthened by adding two knees aft. Finally, a flag locker was installed between the rudder head housing and stern rail, and the timberheads adjacent to the catheads were lengthened.

Changes were also made in *Bounty*'s hold, and here again the draughts are unclear. When Deptford Yard sent the draught of *Bethia* to the Navy Board the yard officers noted, '. . . the Sheer and Decks are agreeable to the Ship as purchas'd, with the several contrivances drawn in Red Ink, the Platforms afore and abaft, &c. in Green are proposed if it meets with your Approval'. Apparently the Navy Board returned *Bounty*'s draught, showing their desired alterations, to the yard, and it is here that the confusion arises; I am uncertain whether the platforms were existing or merely proposed. Most probably the fore platform was in place and held the galley, storerooms and cabins, and the aft platform was at least in place, as there was a ladder leading to it, but not necessarily compartmented with cabins except for a bulkhead aft to form the breadroom. In any event, I have shown *Bounty*'s hold plan as it was, and *Bethia*'s hold plan as it may have been if cabins were placed on both platforms. The Inboard Profile of *Bethia* showing changes made in her hold is based on the assumption that fore and aft platforms and cabins were originally in place.

Oddly enough, *Bethia*'s draughts do not show a hold well. This was a room formed by protective bulkheads that kept stowed items away from the base of the bilge pumps in case emergency access was required. The draught of *Bounty* shows a hold well in place and a shot locker just forward of it.

In his account of the mutiny Bligh tells us of reducing *Bounty*'s ballast:

The next material alteration made in the fitting out was lessening the quantity of iron and other ballast. I gave directions that only 19 tons of iron should be taken on board instead of the customary proportion, which was 45 tons. The stores and provisions I judged would be fully sufficient to answer the purpose of the remainder; for I am of the opinion that many of the misfortunes which attend ships in heavy storms of wind, are occasioned by too much dead weight in their bottoms.

Finally, before leaving Spithead, *Bounty* would have received a coat of paint and had her name painted on the counter.

DECORATION

It is highly unlikely that the Navy Board authorized any changes to *Bounty*'s decoration, and, other than painting the hull, particularly in areas of new work, it would have remained as it was for *Bethia*. The standard hull colours of the day were blue for the plank, black for the wale, and yellow for the trim including plancksheer, rails, stanchions, taffrail and headrails. The deck, masts and yards were left as natural wood and the cabin panelling was painted white.

There are two references to the figurehead; the first, by Bligh, is given in a letter to Sir Joseph Banks in which he notes, '. . . a pretty figurehead of a woman in riding habit'. The second is in Bligh's account of the mutiny, and reads, 'The head of the ship was the figure of a woman, and not ill carved. As we were painting the ship's upper works, I directed this figure to be painted in colours, with which the islanders were much pleased.' (At the time *Bounty* was at Tahiti).

No contemporary drawings or paintings of *Bounty* exist and I have not found any verbal description of her stern decoration, so here I have exercised some licence; the drawings show the stern cove carved in a motif that reflects the ship's name, *Bounty*.

STEERING GEAR

There was nothing out of the ordinary about *Bounty*'s steering gear and apart from coppering the rudder and installing bronze fastenings it was not changed from that of *Bethia*. The rudder itself was made up of two large timbers and was hung on the stern post by means of four large hinges formed by gudgeons on the stern post and pintles on the rudder. A hole was cut in the transom planking, through which the rudder passed, and the two transom timbers on either side of it were spaced to allow the rudder to swing. This hole, known as the helm port, was fitted with a tarred canvas shroud to prevent the sea from washing up into the great cabin. At the level of the upper deck the heads of the stern post and rudder were reinforced with iron bands and both were covered with a wooden housing through which the tiller passed. The tiller was tennoned into the rudder head and the hole in the housing for it was made wide enough athwartships to allow for its sweep, and here again a canvas shroud was employed to keep water out.

The steering wheel was single and sat aft of the mizzen mast; its component parts were carved and turned from hardwood and it had brass reinforcing fittings as required. The tiller was controlled by a single rope wrapped seven or nine times around the drum of the wheel, passed through 10-inch blocks directly below, then led to blocks on either side of the deck, brought aft and finally secured to the tiller. The sweep of the tiller and arrangement of control ropes on the quarter-deck made working on the aft area of the ship awkward at best, and indeed Captain Cook had a platform built over *Endeavour*'s tiller, which was arranged similarly to *Bounty*'s, so that his important passengers could walk comfortably around on the poop.

Immediately ahead of the wheel sat the binnacle, the item of furniture which housed the ship's compasses. It was built of hardwood and besides containing the compasses, one on either side, it held an oil lamp and therefore had a brass chimney on its top. Glass panels were fitted in the binnacle to allow the compasses to be seen, but as the binnacle was lashed to the deck very close to the wheel, it would have been difficult for the helmsman to see in; with the mizzen mast and bitts so close in front it would have been awkward even for the officer of the watch, whose duty it was to monitor the compasses, to see in. All metal fittings of the binnacle and surrounding area were of brass rather than ferrous metal so that the compasses would not be adversely affected.

GROUND TACKLE

As mentioned above, *Bethia*'s anchors came with her when she was bought by the Navy, and it is indicative of their importance that Deptford Yard specifically listed their size and price separately when reporting to the Navy Board:

Anchors propos'd to be purchas'd with her:

	Cwt	qr	lb
Anchor of	13	3	0
	13	3	8
Iron stocked	5	1	0
	2	1	20
	1	3	10

The two 13cwt anchors were wooden stocked bower anchors; one was recovered from Bounty Bay and is now at Pitcairn Island. Its principal dimensions are shown in Table 3.

TABLE 3: **ANCHOR DIMENSIONS**

	ft	in
Length of shank	11	7 (ring to crown)
Circumference of shank	1	7
Between bills	8	0
Breadth of palms	1	7
Diameter of ring	1	10

From the table of anchor dimensions it will be seen that these figures coincide with what was common practice of the day. When leaving Tahiti for the last time Fletcher Christian cut *Bounty*'s anchor cable and 'ran'. This anchor was subsequently dragged for and recovered by *Pandora*, the frigate sent to capture *Bounty*'s mutineers, and as *Pandora* was wrecked on the Great Barrier Reef while returning to England, it is believed that this anchor, the second bower, lies with her remains. *Bounty* carried six anchor cables, each 100 fathoms long.

Bligh makes two interesting notes in *Bounty*'s log concerning the best bower anchor. First, on 4 April 1789 he notes, 'In stowing the best bower anchor the stock broke in the nut and fell overboard, being destroyed by the worms. My sheet anchor had an iron stock for the convenience of carrying it in the chains, and I used it therefore as a small bower; I saved the anchor stock. Ships that come here should have iron stocks.' Then, three days later he notes, 'New stocked the best b[owe]r anchor'.

The three iron-stocked anchors were the stream (5cwt 1qrt 0lb) and two kedges (2cwt 1qrt 20lb, and 1cwt 3qrt 10lb). The sheet anchor that Bligh refers to in the log was the stream, and as it was the next in size after the bowers it was adopted as the sheet. (Larger ships usually carried a total of four wood-stocked anchors.) This stream anchor was carried on the channel and the two kedges were carried in the hold.

It was customary to carry windlasses on smaller ships, particularly merchant vessels, as they could be worked by a relatively small crew. On the other hand, the Navy, with a large pool of manpower to draw from, fitted capstans (often in pairs, one above the other) in their ships. The advantage of a windlass operated by a few men was offset by two negative factors: windlasses were slow in operation and took up a good deal of deck space. Apart from rearranging the belfry, no changes were made to *Bethia*'s windlass after she was bought by the Navy. Note that the draughts clearly show three pawls.

Like the windlass, the capstan was originally fitted to *Bethia* and did not undergo any alteration, but its arrangement is interesting; at this time it was usual to mount the capstan with its spindle stepped on the deck below, but as in *Bounty* there was a companionway immediately under it, this would have been impossible. The spindle was critical in that it provided lateral bracing to the capstan, and if *Bounty*'s capstan merely rotated on a short iron spindle on the upper deck its power would have been greatly reduced. Although proof is impossible, this arrangement nevertheless seems to be the only one possible here, and it must be assumed that the capstan was used for very light work only. Furthermore, *Bethia*'s draught shows a deck locker just aft of the capstan (this may have been removable and indeed was removed for *Bounty*) as well as a 12-inch companionway coaming ahead of it. The opening of the companionway could be closed by placing a grating over it, but the locker, which was 3 feet high, ruins an important working principle of the capstan: that men should be able to walk around it in an unbroken circle.

TABLE 2: **ANCHOR DIMENSIONS Based on Falconer's Dictionary of 1830**

Item	Weight (cwt)	Length of the shank	Length of the flukes	Breadth of the palms	Thickness of the palms	Size of the trend	Size of the small round	Outer diam of the ring	Thickness of the ring
Bowers	14	11ft 8in	3ft 11in	1ft 8¼in	1¼in	4⅞in	4⅜in	1ft 8¼in	2³⁄₁₆in
Stream	6	8ft 6in	2ft 10in	1ft 3in	1in	3¼in	3¼in	1ft 3in	1⅝in
Kedge	2	6ft 6in	2ft 2in	11in	¾in	2¾in	2¼in	11in	1⅛in

Note: The figures given here do not precisely match the weights of *Bounty*'s anchors; they are the next closest size listed by Falconer.

PUMPS

The pumps carried aboard *Bounty* were of the elm tree type; that is, they were made from the trunk of an elm forming a tube that extended from 3 feet above the upper deck to the lowest point of the ship, just aft of the mainmast. They were of a simple design; a handle (or brake) operated a metal rod in the tube of the pump and at the lower end of this rod was a one-way valve made from a perforated disc. As the rod pushed the disc downwards the holes permitted water to pass through, but on the upward stroke a leather flap fell over the holes to prevent the passage of water, thus causing it to be carried upwards. As the stroke of the rod was less than 3 feet, another such valve was placed at the base of the pump, and the pump had to be primed to work. Seepage water was collected in a cistern at the base of the pump by means of holes bored through each frame, and any water that spilled through deck openings into the hold was collected by means of channels, limber passages, running the whole length of the ship on either side of the keelson. At the upper deck the brakes were made removable so as not to interfere with the working of the ship when the pumps were not in use. On large ships this type of pump was not used for pumping bilge water but rather for pumping sea water (used primarily for washing the ship or, if needed, fire fighting) while chain pumps were employed to control seepage.

Bethia's outboard profile does not show pumps (although her upper and lower deck plans do, but not a hold well) but it is difficult to imagine a ship of her size without pumps. In any event, *Bounty* carried two elm tree pumps, aft of the mainmast and roughly 2 feet either side of the centreline.

On *Bounty*'s outward voyage Bligh developed a novel application for the pumps, details of which are given in the log. 'February 7, 1788, Drew the boxes of one pump & employed hands to pour water down, and kept the other pump constantly going for one hour, until the water came out no more offensive than when it was put in'. He found another use for the pumps on 22 February 1788: 'In heavy rains when the ship became heated below I found this to have the most valuable effect and I believe the pumps to be the best ventilators that can be put into a ship'.

BOATS

As originally ordered by the Navy Board on 20 June 1787, while *Bounty* was fitting out, her boats were to be a 20-foot launch, and 18-foot cutter and a 16-foot cutter or jolly boat. These boats were apparently delivered to Deptford Yard but at Bligh's request the first two were exchanged for a 23-foot launch and a 20-foot cutter. Bligh, having had experience in the South Seas, realized the value of large boats for provisioning and watering. The Navy Board's decision that the longest boat was to be of 20 feet was probably arrived at by considering stowage; from *Bounty*'s fore brace bitts to her fore companionway is a little over 18 feet so a 20-foot boat would have fitted quite comfortably on the main hatch. Even after removing her rudder the 23-foot launch took up a

great area of deck space and Bligh states the bow came 'well with the fore hatchway, rather projecting over it'.

The problem of boat stowage does not end with the excessive length of the launch; it is complicated further when we consider height. If *Bounty*'s two largest boats were stowed alongside one another there would have been a mere 2 feet 9 inches between either boat and the rail, and as this area of the ship was important for sail-handling it is likely that the cutter sat in the launch, which was placed on *Bounty*'s centreline. The problem then arises of where to stow the Jolly Boat. Three options are available here: the launch may have been stowed off-centre with the 20-foot cutter within and the Jolly Boat snugged beside it; the three boats may have all been stowed on the centreline of the ship with the Jolly Boat on top (this would have been an awkward balancing act and would interfere with the mainsail); or, when trading *Bounty*'s small boats for larger ones the 16-foot cutter may have been dropped. Whatever the real answer is, I have shown *Bounty* with two boats only.

Bounty's 23-foot launch is as well known as the ship herself due to Bligh's 3600-mile voyage in her. She was carvel built, six-oared, and was designed to carry thirteen people (when Bligh was set adrift there was a total of nineteen in the launch). It is believed that the launch was built by a Mr John Burr, a contractor for Navy boats, at a cost of about £43. As the launch was intended for anchor-handling and other heavy duties she was fitted with a removable windlass amidships and two davits with a sheave were placed in her stern. A standard draught for 23-foot launches of this time exists and shows this outline specification:

Length	23ft 0in
Breadth	6ft 9in
Depth	2ft 9in
Stern sided	0ft 3½in
Keel Do. Midships	0ft 3⅞in
Post sided at the Tuck	0ft 3½in
Alow [below]	0ft 3in
Transom thick	0ft 2in
Floor timbers Sided	0ft 2in
Moulded at the Heads	0ft 2⅛in
Throat	0ft 3⅞in
Futtocks Sided Alow [below]	0ft 2in
Square at the Heads	0ft 1⅞in

We also know that the launch was a good sea boat; Bligh notes in the log, while adrift, '*4 May, 1789* We could do nothing more than keep befor the sea, in the course of which the boat performed so wonderfully well . . .'

The rigging of boats varied quite dramatically and was determined by the intended use of the boat as well as the personal preference of those who sailed them. The draught of *Bounty*'s launch clearly shows provision for stepping one mast, well forward, and in this instance she would most likely have been rigged as a cutter. However, Bligh makes a number of references to her rig in the log that have convinced me that she carried two masts:

3 May 1789   I bore away under a reefed lug fore sail
10 May [1789]   I now got fitted a pair of shrouds to each mast
10 May 1789   In the afternoon I fitted a pair of shrouds for each mast, and contrived a canvas weather cloth round the boat, and raised the quarters about 9 inches, by nailing on the seats of the stern sheets, which proved of great benefit to us.

The drawings show the boat rigged as a lugger, with masts and yards, rigging and sails all based on Steel. As so much variation occurred with boat rigging, the figures given in the Rigging Schedule under 'Rigging for cutter and launch' can only serve as a general guideline.

After carrying Bligh and his followers to Coupang (Kupang) *Bounty*'s launch was towed to Batavia (Jakarta) and eventually sold at auction. By this time Bligh had grown sentimentally attached to her and in his account he wrote, 'The launch was likewise sold. The services she had rendered us, made me feel a great reluctance at parting with her, which I would not have done, if I could have found a convenient opportunity of conveying her to Europe.'

The 20-foot cutter was clinker built, shipped six oars and was designed to carry a maximum of ten men. The drawings show her rigged as a cutter, with a single mast set well forward, a large fore-and-aft main sail spread on a gaff and boom and two fore sails. Here again, rigging and sails are based on Steel's proportions. If *Bounty* carried a 16-foot Jolly Boat, it would have been clinker built and would have carried four oars.

CREW AND ACCOMMODATION
Based on a formula of 15.5 tons per man, *Bethia*, as a merchantman, would have required a crew of some fifteen men to sail her. For the purpose of the Navy's South Sea mission *Bounty*'s total proposed complement was forty-five:

TABLE 4: **SCHEME OF COMPLEMENT**

1	Lieutenant to command	1 Boatswain's mate
1	Master	1 Gunner's mate
1	Boatswain	1 Carpenter's mate
1	Gunner	1 Carpenter's crew
1	Carpenter	1 Sailmaker
1	Surgeon	1 Corporal
2	Master's mates	1 Clerk and steward
2	Midshipmen	25 Able seamen
2	Quartermasters	
1	Quartermaster's mate	45 TOTAL

This complement was altered slightly as an Armourer and an Assistant Gardener were assigned to *Bounty*, so two seamen were dropped to make room for them. When *Bounty* sailed she carried forty-six men, as a Botanist had been assigned; understandably, overcrowding occurred on her lower deck when her crew was increased threefold. This problem was exacerbated by her load of provisions for eighteen months and by the physical alterations to the ship which reduced crew accommodation area.

As the great cabin was given over to the stowage of plant pots, a small sleeping cabin was built for Bligh just ahead of it on the starboard side and a similar cabin was installed for the Master, opposite. Between these cabins was a companionway lobby, and the Captain's dining room with its pantry was placed forward of these. The dining room also served as a day room for Bligh and as an office for the Clerk. As mentioned above, berths formed by canvas screens were placed on either side of the upper deck ahead of the dining room bulkhead for the Master's Mates and Midshipmen. The remainder of the lower deck, a space roughly 22 feet by 36 feet, was allotted to thirty-three seamen, with some of the space also taken up by hatches, companionways and the stove. Bligh refers to the cramped quarters aboard *Bounty* in his account, dated 10 April 1788, '. . . The decks also became so leaky, that I was obliged to allot the great cabin, of which I made little use, except in fine weather, to those people who had wet berths, to hang their hammocks in; and by this means the between decks was less crowded'.

On the aft platform of *Bounty*'s hold, the cockpit, seven small rooms (their headroom being barely 5½ feet between the beams) were built as cabins for the Botanist, Captain's Clerk, Surgeon, Steward and Gunner and as the Captain's store room and slop room. Aft of this platform, in the after peak, was the bread room, and below it were the spirit room, fish room and aft magazine. Cabins for the Boatswain and Carpenter were located on the fore platform as well as their respective store rooms and the Gunner's store room, sail room, pitch room and block room. Below the platform was a second Boatswain's store room and sail room and the forward magazine.

The Navy Board ordered a new firehearth for *Bounty* in July 1787 and it had been installed before undocking on 14 August. This particular firehearth, called a Brodie stove after its manufacturer, had been adopted by the Navy in May 1781 as the only type of firehearth to be employed on His Majesty's ships. (Brodie held this monopoly until 1819.) The stove was built of wrought and cast iron, was fired by coal or wood, and its cooking facilities included a bake oven, boilers and a roasting hearth. A spit was mounted at the front of the roasting hearth on adjustable brackets and it was driven by a chain that was driven in turn by a fan in the chimney. A fresh water condenser was placed on top of the stove, aft, and the stove's metal chimney could be rotated as required by the direction of the wind. While trying to round Cape Horn Bligh notes, 'With so much bad weather, I found it necessary to keep a constant fire, night and day; and one of the watch always attended to dry the people's wet clothes: and this, I have no doubt, contributed to their health as to their comfort'.

One other stove, or space heater, was placed aboard *Bounty*. On 10 October 1787 the Admiralty wrote to the Navy Board,

. . . We do hereby desire and direct you to order a proper stove to be placed in the apartment on board the *Bounty* armed storeship, which is intended to contain the principal part of the Trees and Plants, to prevent their receiving injury from the cold during their passage round the Cape of Good Hope . . .'

MASTS AND YARDS
Details concerning the dimensions of *Bounty*'s masts and yards are we documented as some of her spars were altered twice during refit and propose changes to them were recorded. In Table 5, the first set of figures is for *Beth* as she was bought, as Deptford Yard sent them to the Navy Board on 6 June With these figures came a request for instructions, and on 8 June the Boar ordered that *Bounty*'s masts and yards were to comply with the second set c figures listed. In comparing the two sets of figures we find that the mai topgallant and polehead were reduced, as were the fore topgallant an

TABLE 5: DIMENSIONS OF MASTS AND YARDS

Item	As bought with *Bethia*		As ordered by the Admiralty		As requested by Bligh	
	length	*diam*	*length*	*diam*	*length*	*diam*
Mainmast	58ft 10in	16in	58ft 10in	16in	55ft 0in	16in
Main topmast	35ft 10in	10¾in	35ft 10in	35ft 10¾in	35ft 10in	10¾in
Main topmast head	4ft 9in		4ft 9in		4ft 9in	
Main topgallant mast	23ft 10in	8in	18ft 2in	8in	18ft 2in	6in
Main polehead	10ft 9in		9ft 1in		9ft 1in	
Main yard	40ft 5in	11¼in	46ft 6in	11¾in	41ft 0in	9½in
Main topyard	35ft 2in	8⅛in	35ft 2in	8⅛in	31ft 0in	6½in
Main topgallant yard			24ft 8⅝in	5in	24ft 8in	5in
Foremast	53ft 4in	16½in	53ft 4in	16½in	51ft 0in	16½in
Fore topmast	34ft 3in	10¾in	34ft 3in	10¾in	34ft 3in	10¾in
Fore topmast head	4ft 0in		4ft 0in		4ft 0in	
Fore topgallant mast	23ft 5½in	6in	17ft 3in	4¾in	17ft 3in	4¾in
Fore polehead	12ft 2in		8ft 7in		8ft 7in	
Fore yard	40ft 5in	11in	40ft 5in	10in	38ft 0in	8⅞in
Fore topyard	30ft 6in	7¾in	30ft 6in	7in	28ft 0in	5⅞in
Fore topgallant yard			24ft 8in	5in	24ft 8in	5in
Mizzen mast	48ft 2in	11¼in	48ft 2in	11¼in	48ft 2in	11¼in
Mizzen topmast	24ft 3½in	6⅞in	24ft 3½in	6⅞in	24ft 3½in	6⅞in
Mizzen topmast head	3ft 1in		3ft 1in		3ft 1in	
Mizzen yard (gaff)	21ft 2in	6⅛in	21ft 2in	6⅛in	21ft 2in	6⅛in
Crossjack yard	36ft 2in	7½in	30ft 6in	6½in	30ft 6in	6½in
Mizzen topmast yard	24ft 0in	5¼in	24ft 0in	5in	24ft 0in	5in
Bowsprit	35ft 4in	18¼in	35ft 4in	18¼in	35ft 4in	18¼in
Bowsprit housing	10ft 2in		10ft 2in		10ft 2in	
Jib boom	27ft 1in	8¾in	27ft 1in	8¾in	27ft 1in	8¾in
Spritsail yard			30ft 6in	6⅜in	30ft 6in	6in

polehead; the fore and mizzen topyards were reduced in diameter only, and the crossjack yard was reduced in length and diameter. Furthermore, main and fore topgallant yards were needed (and provided) as was a spritsail yard, and because the main yard was to be increased by some 6 feet, a new one would have had to be provided. This general reduction in top weight was in keeping with Admiralty policy for ships headed to the South Seas.

In the draughts, further changes were made to *Bounty*'s masts and bowsprit; *Bethia*'s draught shows the heels of her masts tennoned directly into the keelson, whereas on *Bounty*'s draught mast steps are clearly shown. The bowsprit was altered in *Bounty* by raising its heel some 8 inches, thus reducing its steeve.

The second alteration to *Bounty*'s rig was the result of Bligh's request and was prompted by his knowledge of the South Seas. He notes in his account, 'The ship was masted according to the proportion of the navy; but on my application, the masts were shortened, as I thought them too much for her, considering the nature of the voyage'. Dimensions of *Bounty*'s masts and yards as she left Spithead, those reflecting Bligh's wish, are given in the third set of figures; by comparison of these with those of the Admiralty we find that the main and fore masts, yards and topsail yard were all reduced. The note in the log concerning this work reads, 'On the 4th September from an application I had made the lower masts were got out and shortened and the lower topsail yards were cut on shore agreeable to my request'.

Shortening a mast would have involved a good deal of work, as all of the rig above it (starting with the sails, then yards, running rigging, top and topgallant masts and their standing rigging) would have to be brought down; the mast would then be lifted, shortened, retennoned, replaced and rerigged, with adjustments to the standing rigging as required. This was not an uncommon practice and was even done away from docking facilities; indeed, Bligh, while at False Bay, had *Bounty*'s mizzen mast cut down; '26 May, 1788, I directed that the Mizzen Mast should be raised out of the step and two feet cut off it, as it is too taut and strains the ship about the quarter and it was done and the rigging repaired and fitted'. Similarly, shortening a yard would not be just a matter of cutting a length off each end; the whole yard would have to be retapered to suit. This was of particular importance when lower and topyards were involved, as quarter irons and boom irons had to be refitted.

As well as asking that the *Bounty*'s spars be reduced, Bligh also asked for 'Gratten Tops' (grating tops) as opposed to the plank tops that were used by the Navy as fighting platforms. It was customary for merchant vessels to carry grating tops, (that is, tops whose platforms were formed by grating) as they were not required for martial activities and they were lighter and less subject to rot than plank. It may have been that *Bethia*'s tops had been changed to plank, or perhaps the Navy Board was contemplating doing so.

The drawings show *Bounty*'s masts and yards with lengths and given diameters taken from the last set of dimensions. All other dimensions and diameters are based on Steel's formulae for mastmaking and as such cannot be too far from wrong, since Steel's book came only seven years after *Bounty*'s refit. Generally, *Bounty*'s spars are slightly larger than as required by Steel for their length and it is interesting that *Bethia*'s foremast was half an inch larger in diameter than her main. Finally, I have shown the lower mast bibbs in the style of the merchant navy, fixed to the sides of the hounds and not tennoned to their fore faces, as in all likelihood *Bethia*'s masts were built this way and there was no need for the Navy to change them.

SAILS

Bounty was fully rigged as a ship; that is, she carried square sails on all three masts. Although this point is quite obvious it is worth mentioning, as her size makes her rig somewhat unusual, in that vessels of less than 250 tons were customarily rigged fore-and-aft. Generally, the fore-and-aft rig required less manpower per ton to handle and this was an important consideration for merchantmen.

Square sails carried on *Bounty* were: spritsail on the bowsprit; course, topsail and topgallant sail on the foremast; course, topsail and topgallant sail on the mainmast; and topsail on the mizzen mast. Fore-and-aft sails, also known as staysails, were: three between the bowsprit and foremast; three between the fore- and mainmasts; two between the main and mizzen masts and the very important mizzen course, or driver, on the mizzen. She also set three studding sails on either side of the fore- and mainmasts, to bring the total number of sails to twenty-nine. A matching suit of spare sails was carried in the hold.

Here again, the drawings show the sails in accordance with Steel, with sizes determined from the sail and rigging drawings, and they are based on masts and yards as carried on *Bounty* when she left Spithead. If *Bethia* was fitted with sails when she was purchased by the Navy, they would have been modified to suit the new spar dimensions (or she would have been fitted with new ones); it seems that further changes were still necessary, as Bligh notes that, 'The lower studding sails being too deep I cut them and made royals out of the canvas'. Royal sails would have been roughly 7 feet by 21 feet for the fore polemast and 8 feet by 22 feet for the main.

RIGGING

Any difference between *Bethia*'s and *Bounty*'s rigging would be minimal, if there was a difference at all, and as *Bounty* was rerigged to suit the new spar configuration, it is safe to assume that her rigging met with Navy standards. As the smallest ship listed by Steel is of 250 tons (ships from eighteen to fourteen guns, or from 300 to 250 tons), the rigging schedule shows rope sizes (circumference) as given for this ship, and as such some items, particularly the largest, may be slightly oversize. I have, however, made adjustments where Steel's list is obviously inaccurate. The lengths of rigging are determined somewhat differently as a rope's length was calculated by a formula based on its respective spar's length. These lengths may not be perfectly accurate as I believe they were mainly used as a guideline for the ropemakers; minor adjustments would have been made by the ship's riggers. This would not apply to a re-rig, in which a rope being replaced could be measured.

Some rigging items are not given by Steel for a ship of *Bounty*'s tonnage and where this is the case I have used other means to determine their sizes and lengths. Some of these items include wooldings, bowsprit gammoning, jib-boom lashing and strap, Flemish horses and some studding sail rigging. Figures given for shrouds and swifters by Steel are based on seven pairs, and as *Bounty* carried five pairs, an adjustment was made which has also affected the overall length of ratlines. Royal backstays and flagstaff stays are not shown by Steel as he does not allow for royal sails. I have shown these items, although they were unlikely to have been in place when *Bounty* left Spithead, as Bligh would have rigged them when setting new royals. Also, running rigging to the royals must be allowed for.

Finally, after allowing that *Bounty* was somewhat out of the ordinary for the Navy, the belaying plan has been arranged to follow conventions of the day as closely as possible.

ORDNANCE

Although *Bounty* carried four 4-pounder guns (short) and ten half-pounder swivels she could not, by any definition, be termed a fighting ship. *Bounty* mounted guns for two reasons: first as a deterrent to pirates (who were often found on the eastern seas) and any hostile natives who might be encountered;

and second to salute another ship or when entering port.

Bounty's 4-pounder guns were the standard design Naval gun, and as such they were mounted on wooden carriages. The 4-pounder given in the drawing is based on the dimensions of one of *Endeavour*'s guns which Captain Cook was forced to jettison when his ship struck the Great Barrier Reef. This gun is now in Australia and would have been virtually identical to *Bounty*'s; it is 6 feet long, 13½ inches in diameter at its breech, its bore is 3¼ inches and it weighs about 1000 pounds. A crew of four men was required to work this gun and it is interesting to note that on *Bounty* there is a shroud deadeye directly in front of the first gunport and a timberhead just inboard of the second. Furthermore, the recoil of the second gun was seriously impeded by the mizzen topsail sheet bitts. These obstructions would have been a problem in a real man-of-war.

Swivel guns were the smallest mounted weapons to be employed by Naval ships; they were used for anti-personnel purposes and were manned by a crew of two. They were mounted by means of a wrought iron yoke that was clamped around the trunnions and had a spike fitted to it. The spike (the term spike is somewhat misleading as it was really a spindle) was placed in a hole bored in the top of the timber gun stanchion, and this simple arrangement not only allowed the gun to be trained and elevated, but also made the weapon very portable; swivels were usually carried in the hold until needed. The swivel shown here is 2 feet 9½ inches long, 6½ inches in diameter at the breech, its bore is 1¾ inches and it weighs slightly more than 100 pounds. A lever, known as the tiller, was often fixed to the breech of swivel guns to provide more control when training. Many variations of the tiller occur, but basically, if it had not been cast together with the gun, it was a wrought iron handle that was clamped around the pommelion, and it was about 12 inches long. It is probable that *Bounty*'s swivels were equipped with tillers, but for want of positive information the drawings do not show one.

SOURCES AND BIBLIOGRAPHY

The Admiralty Draughts, National Maritime Museum, Greenwich

Batchelor, N 'HM Armed Vessel *Bounty* (1787)' Model Shipwright No 12, 1975

Barrow, J *The Munity of the* Bounty (edited by Gavin Kennedy), Russell Sharp, 1980

Bligh, W *The Log of the* Bounty, Genesis Publications
  The Log of the Bounty, Golden Cockerel Press
  The Mutiny on Board HMS Bounty, Signet Classic, 1962

Knight, C 'HM Armed Vessel *Bounty*' Mariner's Mirror Vol 22, No 2, Apr 1936

Harland, J *Seamanship in the Age of Sail*, Conway Maritime Press, 1985

Marden, L 'The *Bounty*: Mutiny in the South Seas', *Men, Ships and the Sea*, National Geographic Society, 1973

McGowan, A *The Ship: The Century Before Steam*, Her Majesty's Stationery Office, 1980

Monfeld, W *Historic Ship Models*, Sterling Publications, 1986

Steel, D *Elements of Mastmaking, Sailmaking and Rigging*, Edward W Sweetman, 1982

The Photographs

There are no authentic contemporary models of *Bounty*. The photographs in this section show the two full-scale replicas of the ship used for the 1962 and 1979 recreations for the cinema of Bligh's famous voyage. Both replicas were built to a very high standard, and, in external appearance at least, provide a very good overall impression of the original ship. Deck fittings and internal appearance, however, are not entirely authentic on these replicas, and views of such features have necessarily been kept to a minimum here. The photographs of the earlier replica shown here, built by the Smith & Rhuland Shipyard, Lunenburg, were taken by John Mannering; those of the later replica are courtesy of Mike Davidson of Bounty Voyages Pty of Australia.

2. The more modern replica of *Bounty* was launched in 1979 in New Zealand. She is seen here from the port bow.

3. The replica of 1979 under full sail.

5. Apart from the clothes of the crew members, this view of the 1979 replica gives a good impression of the deck of the original ship.

4. A port quarter view of the 1979 replica.

6. *Above right:* This port quarter view of the earlier *Bounty* replica, apart from the large number of modern passengers, shows the authenticity of the first reconstruction.

7. A port bow view of the 1962 replica.

8. The earlier replica tied up at Calais. The large lettering on the transom giving the ship's name and her place of construction is not authentic.

9. A close-up of the figurehead of the earlier replica; the original was described by Bligh as 'a pretty figurehead of a woman in riding habit'.

10. The 1979 replica under full sail in the Hauraki Gulf, New Zealand, in 1981.

12. The fore course of the 1979 replica, seen from the deck looking forward.

11. A deck view forward on the starboard side of the more recent replica, showing the main shrouds.

13. A detail view of the main lower mast head rigging on the 1979 replica.

The Drawings

Large scale copies of the drawings reproduced in this book can be obtained from the author. Details from: John McKay, PO Box 752, Fort Langley, British Columbia, Canada V0X 1J0.

A General arrangement and lines

A1 GENERAL ARRANGEMENT

A1/1 Isometric view (no scale)

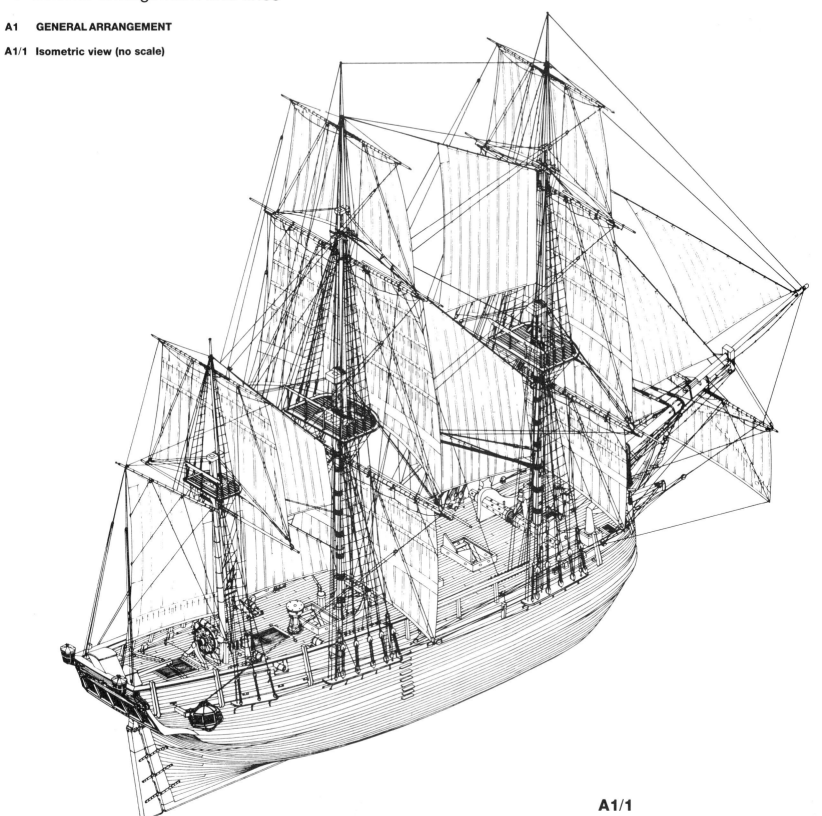

A1/1

A General arrangement and lines

A2   LINES

A2/1 Body plan (1/96 scale)

A2/2 Half breadth plan (1/96 scale)

A2/3 Isometric of body lines – from forward, port (no scale)

A2/4 Isometric of body lines – from aft, starboard (no scale)

A2/1

A2/4

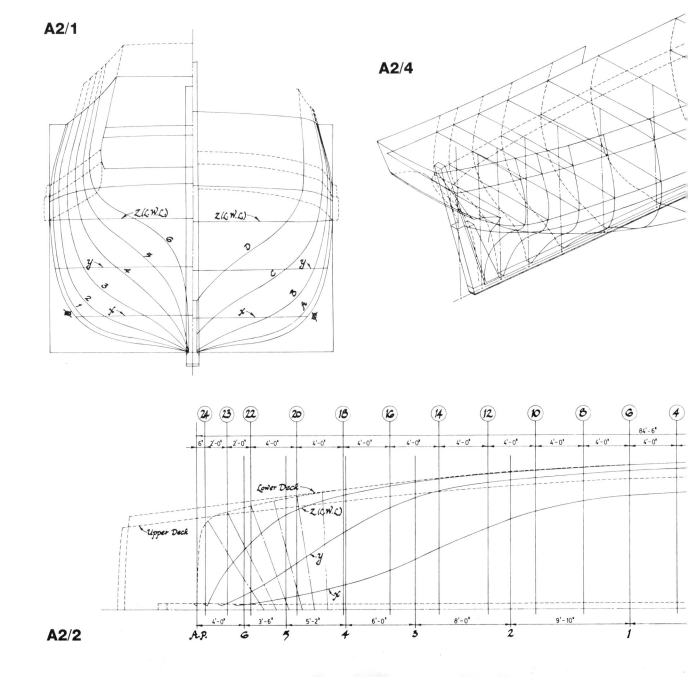

A2/2

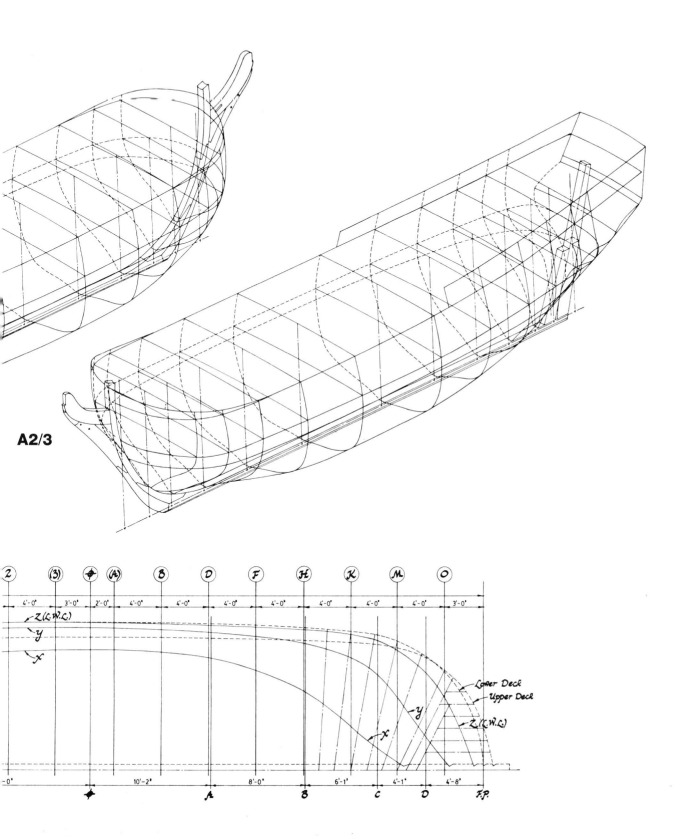

A2/3

A General arrangements

A3   PROFILES AND SECTIONS

A3/1 Outboard profile (1/96 scale)

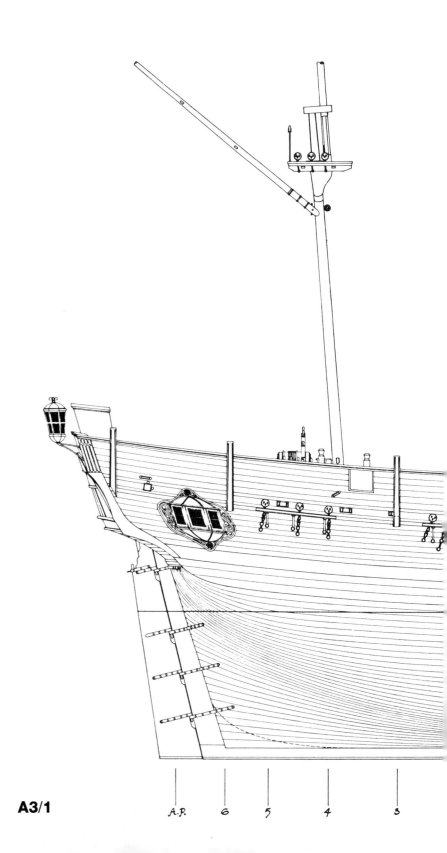

A3/1

A.P.   6   5   4   3

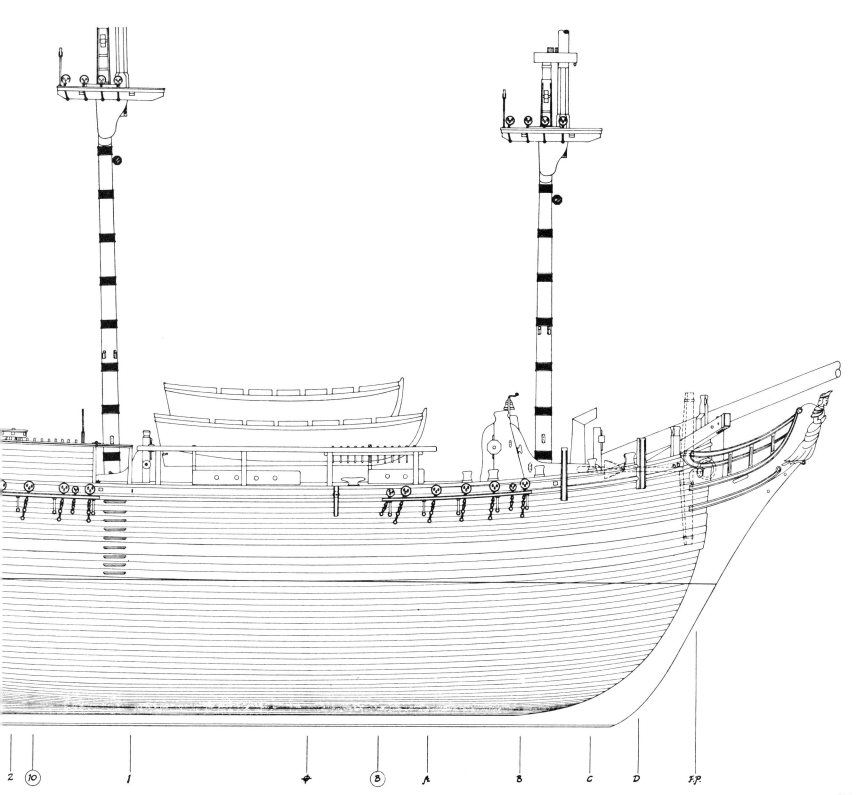

2 ⑩ 1 ⊕ Ⓑ A B C D F.P.

27

A General arrangement and lines

A3/2 Outboard profile of *Bethia*
(1/96 scale)

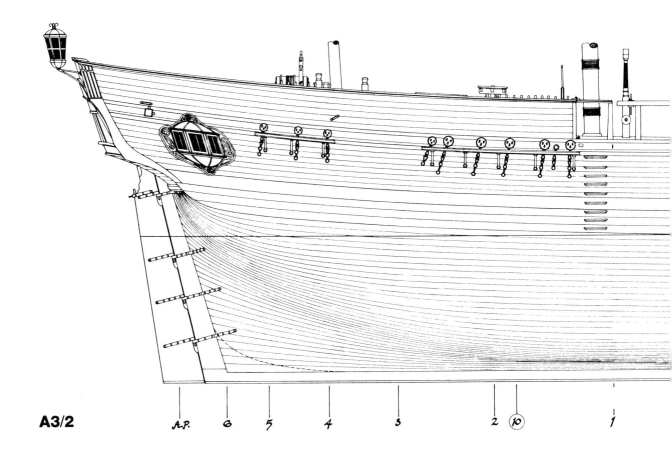

A3/2   A.P.   6   5   4   3   2   10   1

28

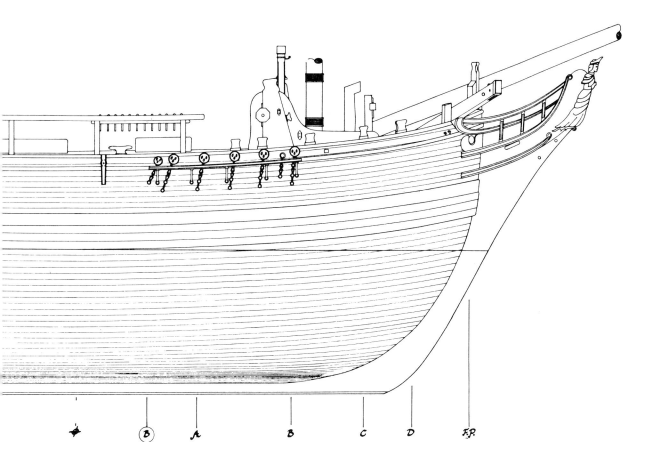

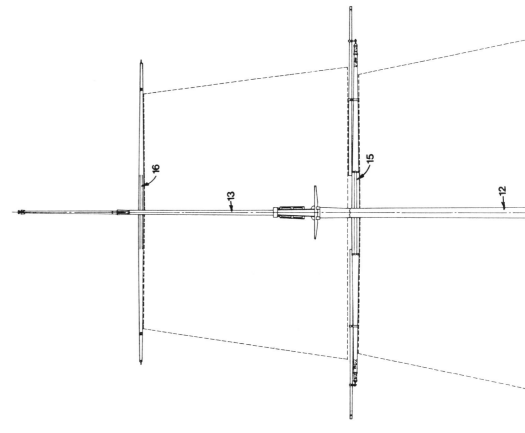

**A3/3 Cross section at 'B' (foremast)
looking forward (1/96 scale)**

1. Forecastle
2. Lower deck
3. Hold
4. Swivel stanchion
5. Carrick bitts
6. Galley stove chimney
7. Galley stove
8. Boatswain's cabin
9. Carpenter's cabin
10. Sail room
11. Fore mast
12. Fore topmast
13. Fore topgallant mast
14. Fore yard
15. Fore topyard
16. Fore topgallant yard

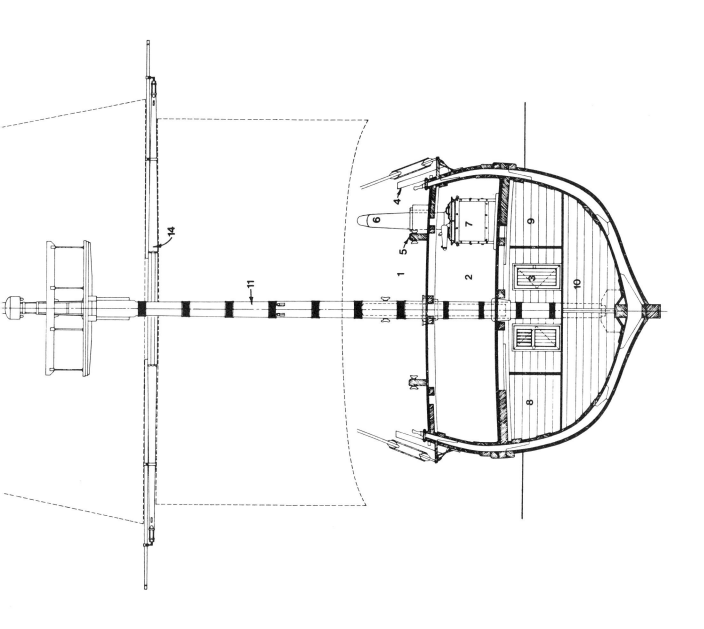

A3/3

A General arrangement and lines

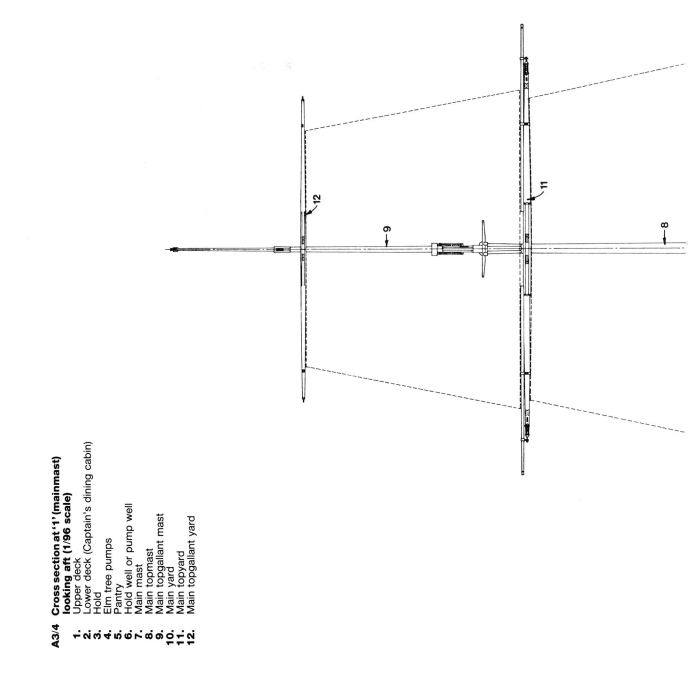

A3/4 Cross section at '1' (mainmast) looking aft (1/96 scale)
1. Upper deck
2. Lower deck (Captain's dining cabin)
3. Hold
4. Elm tree pumps
5. Pantry
6. Hold well or pump well
7. Main mast
8. Main topmast
9. Main topgallant mast
10. Main yard
11. Main topyard
12. Main topgallant yard

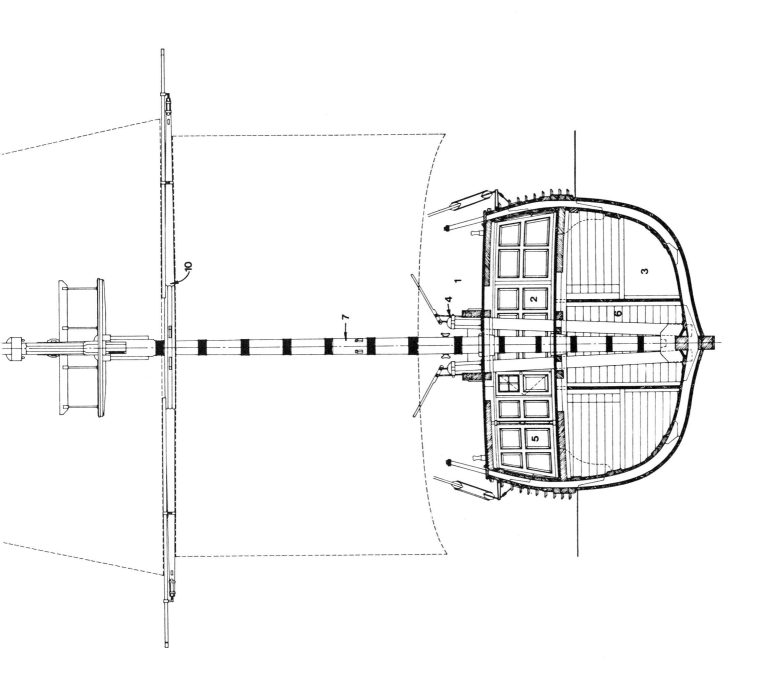

A3/4

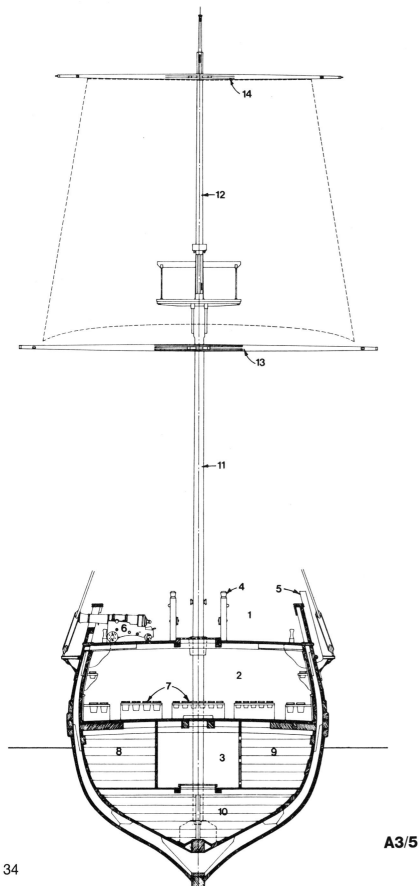

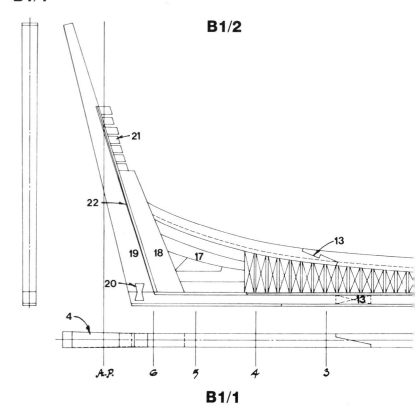

**A3/5 Cross section at '3' (mizzen mast)
looking aft (1/96 scale)**

1.   Quarter deck
2.   Lower deck (garden)
3.   Hold
4.   Mizzen topsail sheet bitts
5.   Swivel stanchion
6.   4-pounder gun
7.   Pot racks
8.   Gunner's cabin
9.   Surgeon's cabin
10. Fish room
11. Mizzen mast
12. Mizzen topmast
13. Crossjack yard
14. Mizzen topyard

B1/4

B1/2

B1/1

A3/5

B Hull construction

B1 KEEL

B1/1 Keel plan (1/96 scale)
1. Cutwater
2. Stem
3. Keel (note scarphs)
4. Stern post

B1/2 Keel elevation (1/96 scale)
1. Gammoning piece
2. Lacing or main piece
3. Chock piece
4. Gripe
5. Upper piece of stem
6. Middle piece of stem
7. Lower piece of stem
8. Upper piece of apron
9. Middle piece of apron
10. Lower piece of apron
11. Deadwood
12. Keelson
13. Scarphs
14. Line of ceiling
15. Keel
16. Square frames
17. Deadwood
18. Inner stern post
19. Stern post
20. Fish plate (copper)
21. Transoms (7 in number)
22. Rabbet
23. False keel

B1/3 Stem, view from forward (1/96 scale)

B1/4 Sternpost, view from aft (1/96 scale)

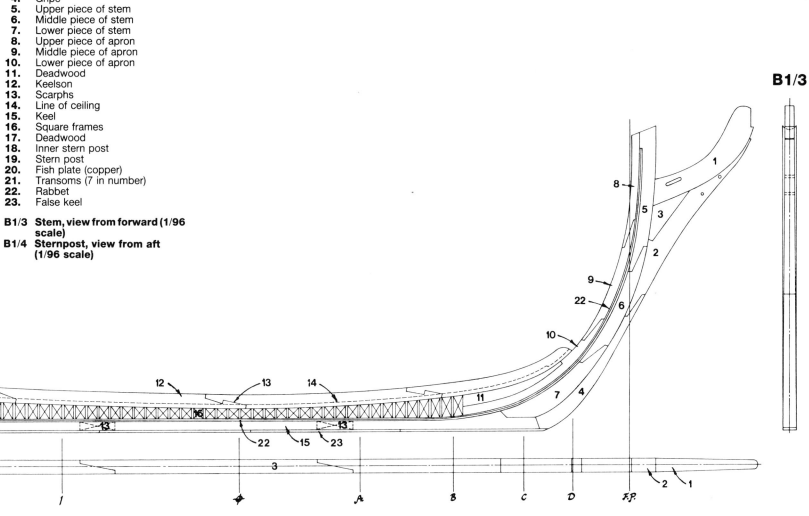

B1/3

B Hull construction

B1/5 Isometric showing keel construction (no scale)

1. Cutwater
2. Stem
3. Apron
4. Rabbet
5. Deadwood
6. False keel
7. Keel
8. Square frames
9. Keelson
10. Inner stern post
11. Stern post
12. Transoms
13. Fish plate

B1/6 Keel detail at fore deadwood, keel detail at square frame, keel detail at aft deadwood (no scale)

1. Keel
2. False keel
3. Deadwood
4. Keelson
5. Limber board
6. Limber strake
7. Ceiling
8. Garboard strake
9. External planking
10. Cant frame
11. Square frame

B1/6

B1/5

B3 STERN

B3/2 Stern transoms – 1 to 7 (1/96 scale)

B3/2

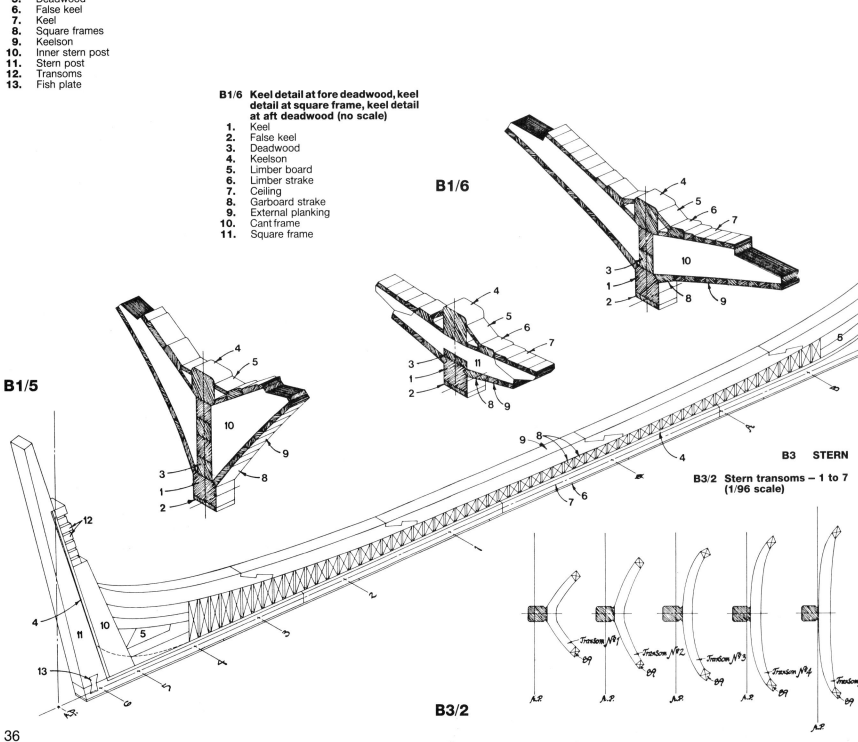

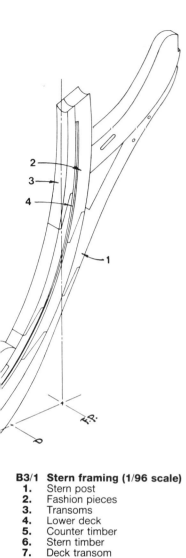

B2 BOW

B2/1 Bow framing (1/96 scale)
1. Stem
2. Knighthead
3. Hawse frames
4. Cant frame
5. Bowsprit
6. Hawse hole
7. Load waterline
8. Profile at dead flat

B2/2 Sketch of bow framing (no scale)

B2/1

B2/2

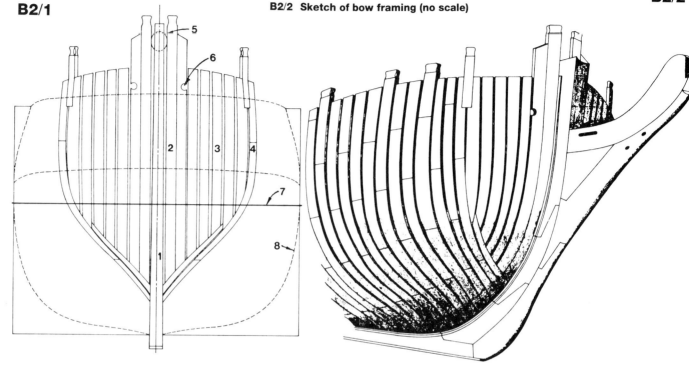

B3/1 Stern framing (1/96 scale)
1. Stern post
2. Fashion pieces
3. Transoms
4. Lower deck
5. Counter timber
6. Stern timber
7. Deck transom
8. Upper deck
9. Load waterline
10. Profile at dead flat

B3/1

B3/3 Sketch of stern framing (no scale)

B3/3

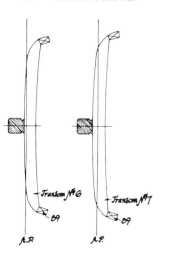

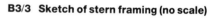

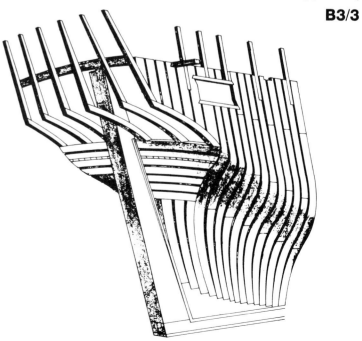

B Hull construction

B4 FRAMES

B4/1 Framing plan (1/96 scale)
1. Cutwater
2. Stem
3. Apron
4. Mast step
5. Keelson
6. Stern post
7. Wing transom and transoms – seven in number
8. Frames:
   numbers 1 to 7 – hawse pieces
   numbers 8 to 19 – cant frames (bow)
   numbers 20 to 78 – square frames
   numbers 79 to 89 – cant frames (stern)
   numbers 90 to 92 – fashion and filling pieces

B4/2 Room and space detail (1/32 scale)

B4/3 Outboard profile: framing (1/96 scale)
1. Cutwater
2. Stem
3. Knighthead
4. Rabbet
5. Keel
6. Stern post
7. Transoms
8. Counter timber
9. Stern timber
10. Frames
11. Opening for quarter gallery
12. Timber heads
13. Stanchion
14. Gunport
15. Air scuttle

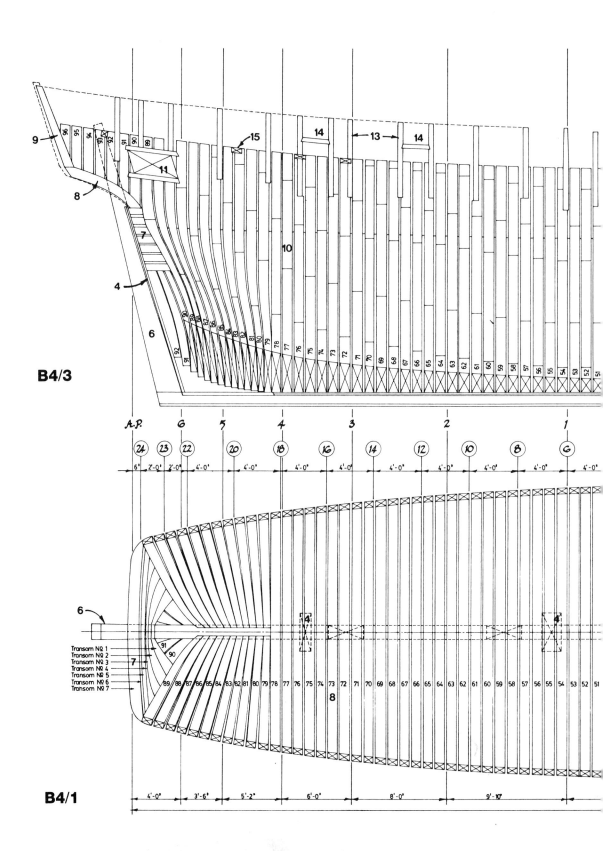

B4/3

B4/1

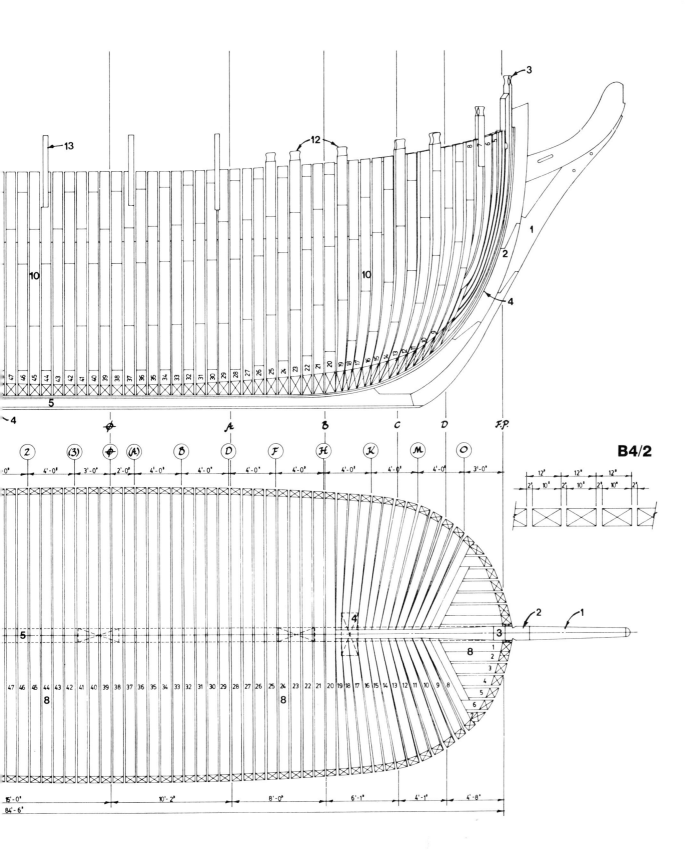

B4/2

B Hull construction

B4/4 Isometric showing framing (no scale)

1. Cutwater
2. Knighthead
3. Hawse pieces
4. Hawse hole
5. Frames
6. Keel
7. Keelson
8. Stanchion
9. Deadwood
10. Fashion pieces
11. Stern post
12. Transoms

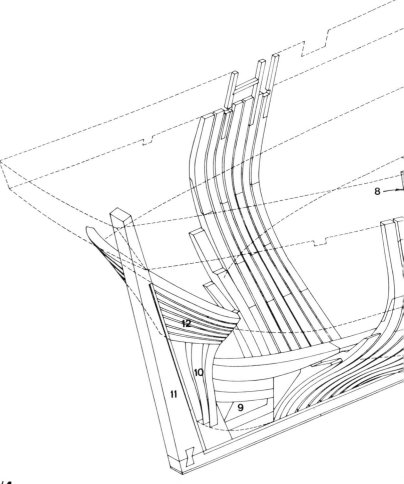

B4/4

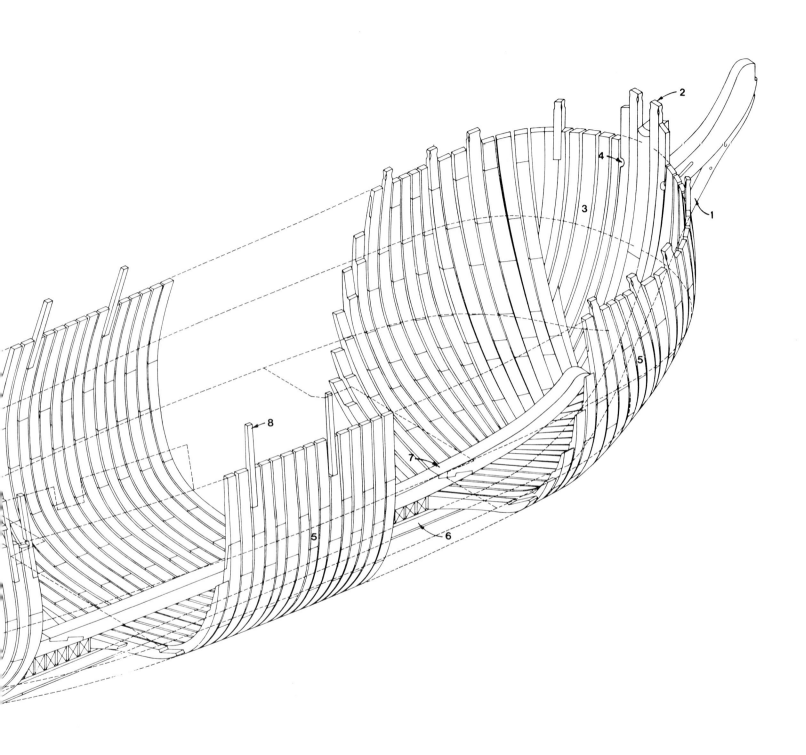

B Hull construction

B5   **PLANKS**

B5/1 **Isometric showing wales and
        planking (no scale)**
  1. Frames
  2. Wale
  3. Keel
  4. Keelson
  5. Mast steps
  6. Deck clamp
  7. Waterway plank
  8. Spirketing
  9. Lining or quickwork
 10. Ceiling
 11. Stern post
 12. Transoms
 13. Counter timbers
 14. Stern timber

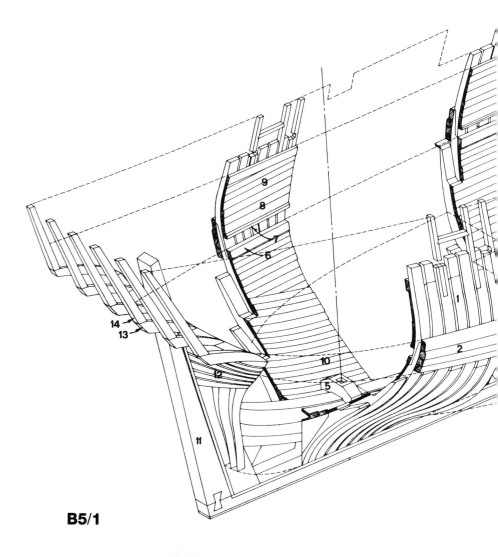

B5/1

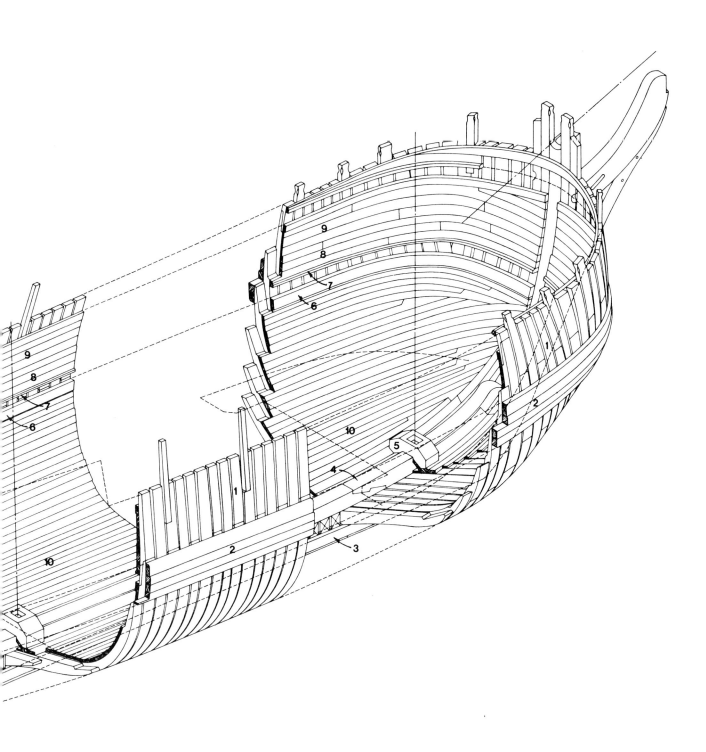

B Hull construction

B6 **BEAMS**

B6/1 **Isometric showing deck beams (no scale)**
1. Wale
2. External planking
3. Keel
4. Keelson
5. Limber board
6. Limber strake
7. Mast steps
8. Frames
9. Deck beams
10. Hold platform beams
11. Breast hook
12. Fore and aft carlings
13. Athwartship carlings (ledges)
14. Lodging knee
15. Hanging knee
16. Stern post
17. Fashion pieces
18. Transoms
19. Counter timbers
20. Stern timbers
21. Deck transom

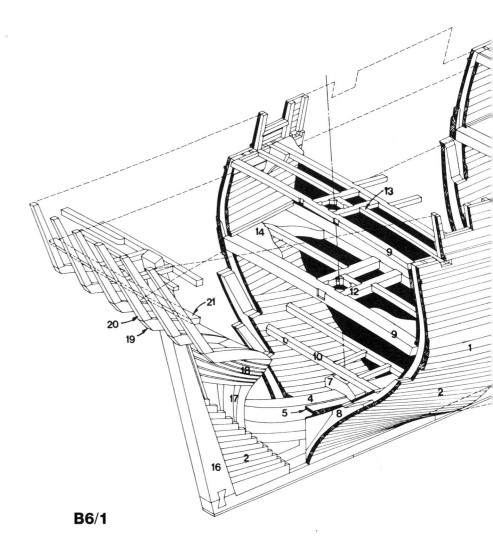

B6/1

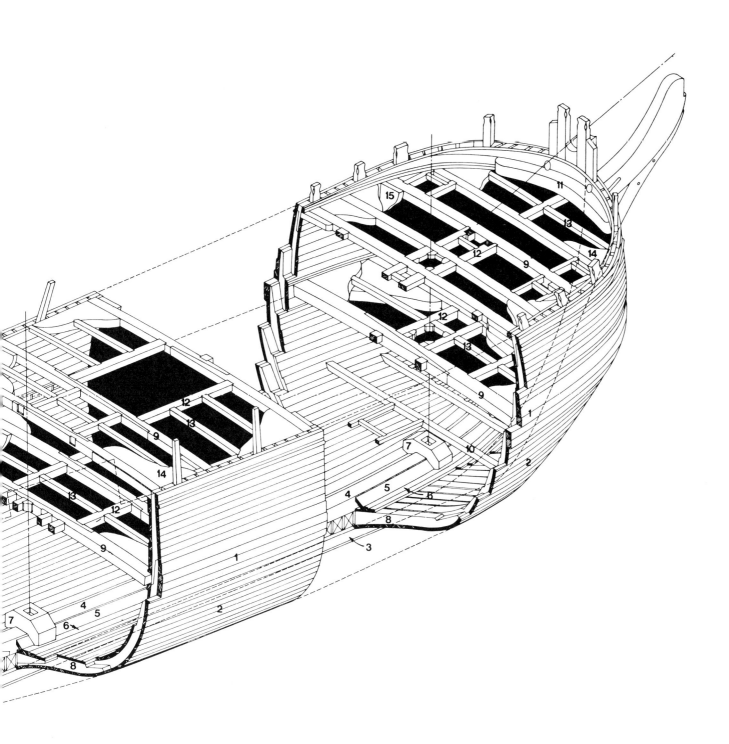

B Hull construction

B7   DECKS

**B7/1 Isometric showing decks
       (no scale)**
1.   External planking
2.   Wale
3.   Frames
4.   Keel
5.   Keelson
6.   Mast steps
7.   Bowsprit
8.   Foremast
9.   Mainmast
10. Mizzen mast
11. Breast hook
12. Forecastle
13. Upper deck
14. Quarterdeck
15. Lower deck
16. Forward hold platform
17. Hold
18. Aft hold platform
19. Stern post
20. Transoms
21. Counter timbers
22. Stern timbers
23. Deck transoms

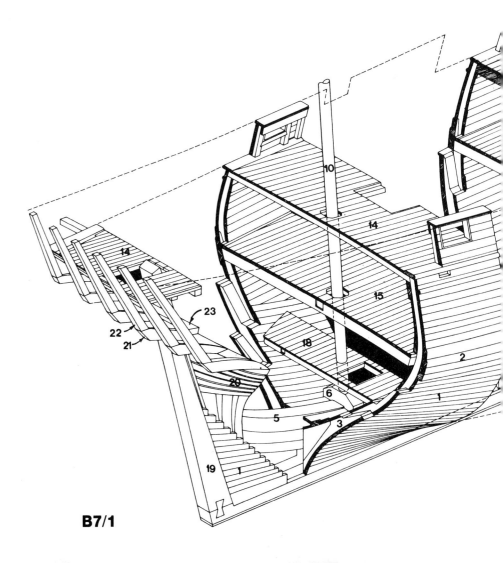

B7/1

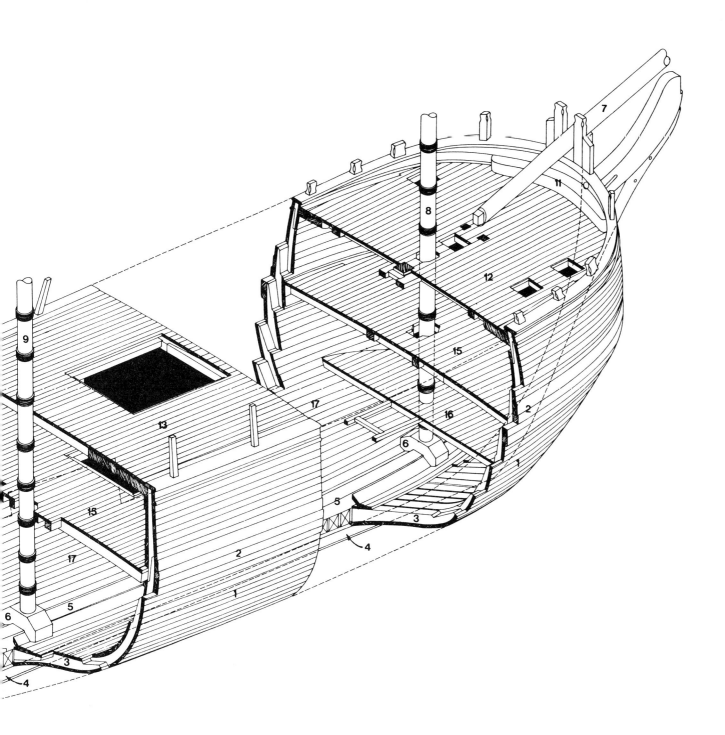

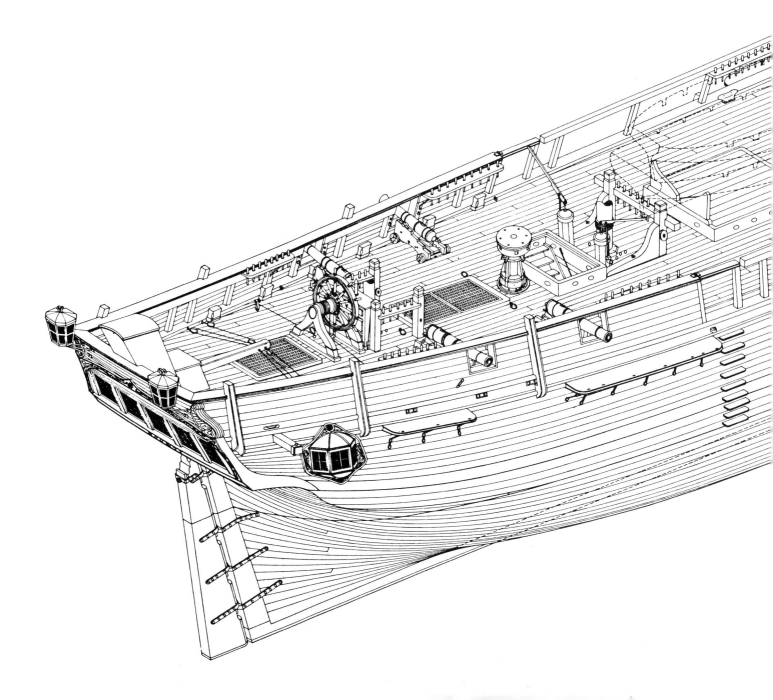

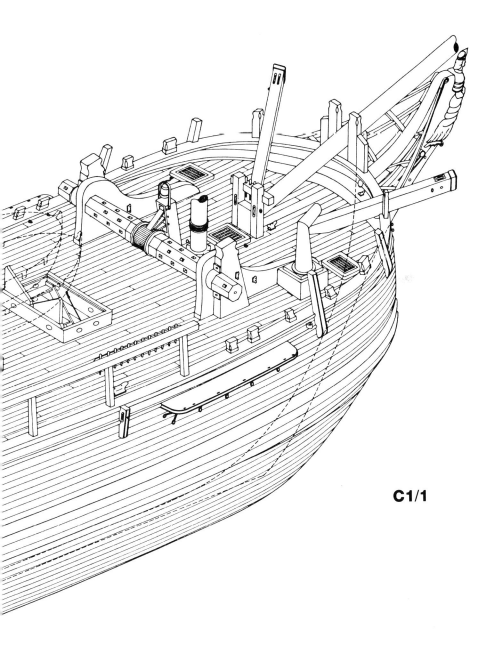

C1/1

C External hull

C1/2 Isometric of the completed hull
(no scale)

C1/2

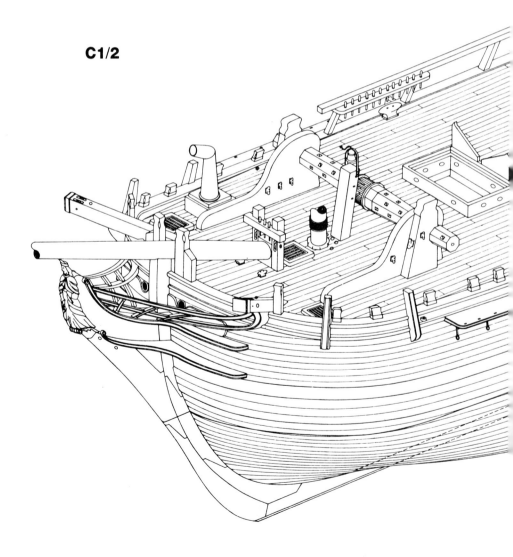

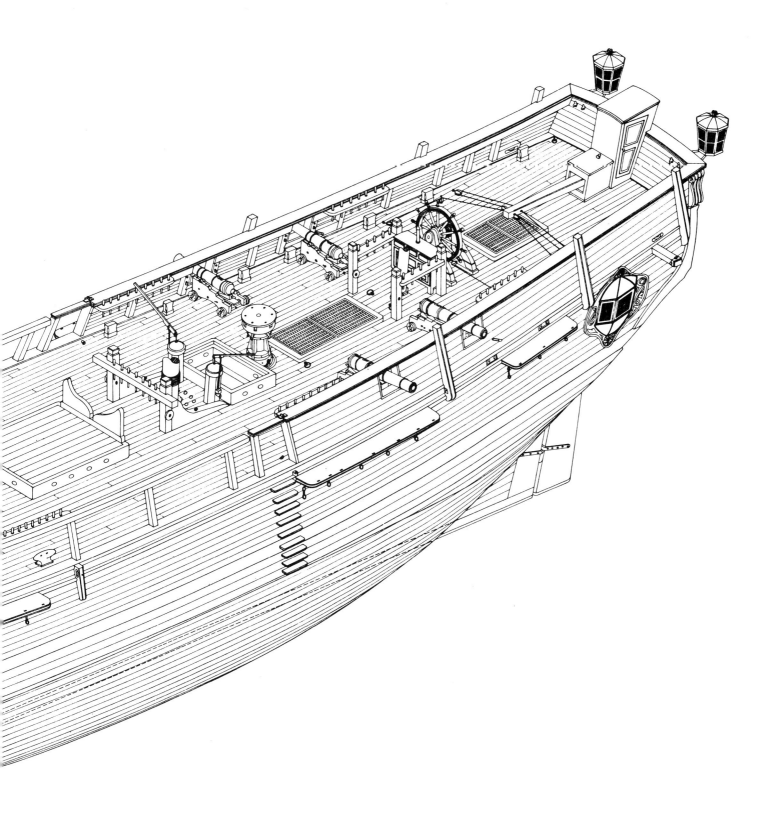

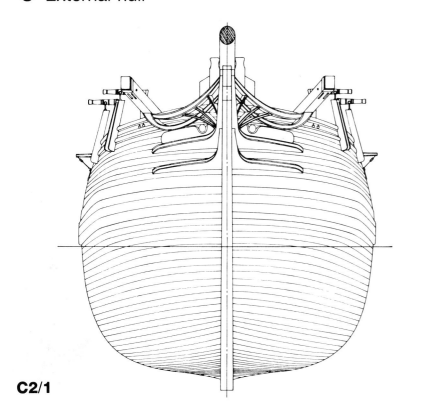

C2/1

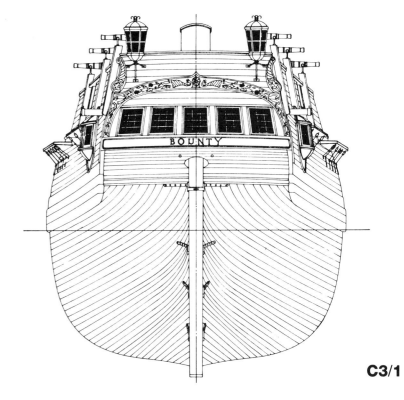

C3/1

C2	BOW	C3	STERN
C2/1	Bow elevation (1/96 scale)	C3/1	Stern elevation (1/96 scale)
C2/2	Sketch of bows (no scale)		
C2/3	Figurehead (no scale)		

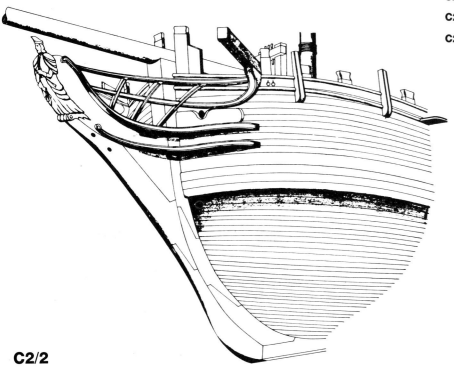

C2/2

C2/3

C3/2

C3/2 Stern decoration (1/48 scale)

C3/3 Stern detail (1/48 scale)
1. Compartmented flag locker
2. Rudder head housing
3. Tiller
4. Quarterdeck
5. Stern post shroud
6. Pannelling
7. Wing transom
8. Lower deck
9. Rudder head
10. Stern post
11. Rudder
12. Counter timber
13. Stern window
14. Stern timber
15. Stern decoration
16. Taffrail
17. External planking

C3/3

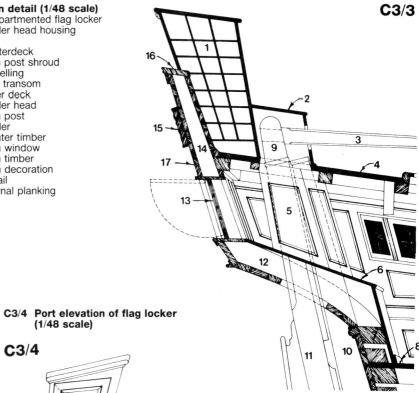

C3/5 Sketch of stern (no scale)

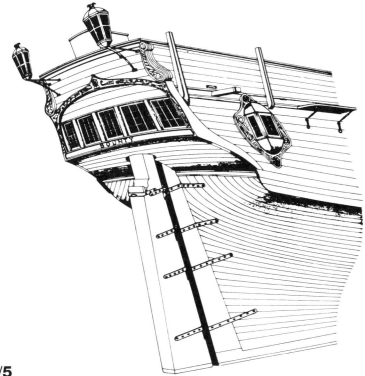

C3/5

C3/4 Port elevation of flag locker (1/48 scale)

C3/4

C3/6 Quarter gallery (no scale)

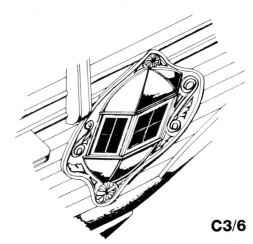

C3/6

C External hull

C4/1
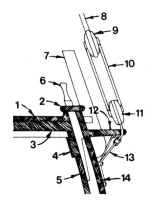

C4/2
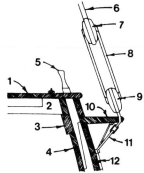

C4/3
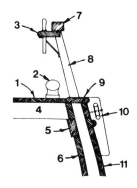

C4/4
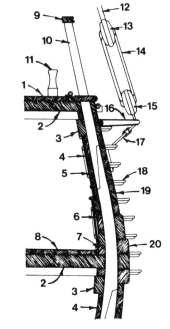

C4   RAIL DETAILS

C4/1   Rail detail at station 'B'
(1/48 scale)
1. Forecastle deck
2. Planksheer rail
3. Lodging knee
4. Deck clamp
5. Lining or quickwork
6. Timber head
7. Swivel stanchion
8. Shroud
9. Shroud deadeye
10. Lanyard
11. Chain deadeye
12. Fore channel
13. Chain
14. External planking

C4/2   Rail detail at station 'A'
(1/48 scale)
1. Upper deck
2. Beam
3. Deck clamp
4. Lining or quickwork
5. Timber head
6. Shroud
7. Shroud deadeye
8. Lanyard
9. Chain deadeye
10. Fore channel
11. Chain
12. External planking

C4/3   Rail detail at station   B
(1/48 scale)
1. Upper deck
2. Cleat
3. Fore pin rail
4. Beam
5. Deck clamp
6. Lining or quickwork
7. Rail
8. Stanchion
9. Planksheer
10. Chesstree
11. External planking

C4/4   Rail detail at station '1'
(1/48 scale)
1. Upper deck
2. Lodging knee
3. Deck clamp
4. Cabin panelling
5. Lining or quickwork
6. Spirketing
7. Waterway plank
8. Lower deck
9. Rail
10. Stanchion
11. Cleat
12. Shroud
13. Shroud deadeye
14. Lanyard
15. Chain deadeye
16. Main channel
17. Chain
18. Side ladder
19. External planking
20. Wale

C4/5   Rail detail at station '2'
(1/48 scale)
1. Upper deck
2. Beam
3. Deck clamp
4. Lining or quickwork
5. Cabin panelling
6. Cleat
7. Main pin rail
8. Planksheer rail
9. Planksheer
10. Main channel

C4/6   Rail detail at station '2'
(1/48 scale)
1. Upper deck
2. Beam
3. Deck clamp
4. Lining or quickwork
5. Cabin panelling
6. Cleat
7. Gun port
8. Planksheer rail
9. Planksheer
10. Main channel
11. Rings for gun tackles

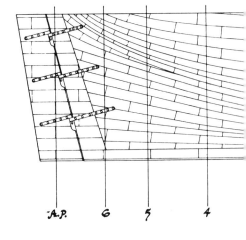

C4/5

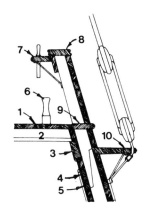

C4/6

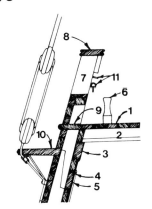

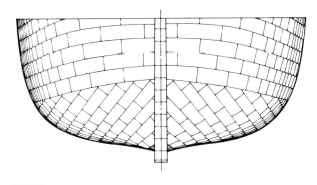

C5/2

C5   **COPPER SHEATHING**

C5/1 Outboard (1/96 scale)

C5/2 Bow (1/96 scale)

C5/3 Stern (1/96 scale)

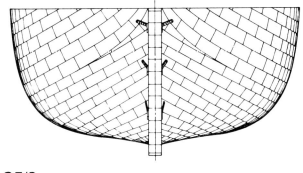

C5/3

C5/1

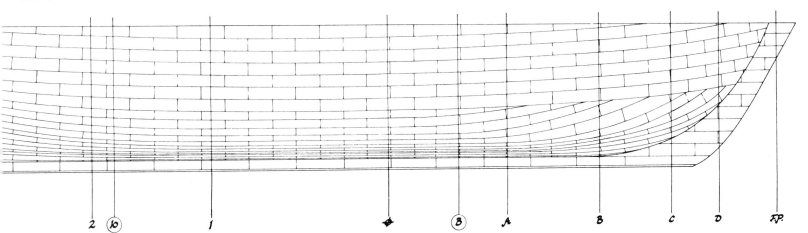

D Internal hull

D1 GENERAL ARRANGEMENT

D1/1 Inboard profile (1/96 scale)

1. Upper deck
2. Lower deck
3. Hold
4. Fore platform
5. Aft platform
6. Bowsprit
7. Knighthead
8. Figurehead
9. Head rails
10. Cutwater
11. Keel
12. Frames
13. Deadwood
14. Stern post
15. Inner stern post
16. Rudder
17. Cathead
18. Half-pounder swivel
19. Fore topsail sheet bitts
20. Foremast
21. Pawl bitt post
22. Windlass
23. Bell
24. Fore pin rail
25. Rail
26. Boat chock
27. Companionway
28. Main hatch
29. Fore brace bitts
30. Mainmast
31. Pump
32. Main pin rail
33. Capstan
34. Mizzen topsail sheet bitts
35. Poop pin rail
36. Mizzen mast
37. Steering wheel
38. Tiller
39. Flag locker
40. Stern lantern
41. Galley stove (starboard)
42. Fore hatch
43. Captain's dining cabin
44. Garden (great cabin)
45. Rudder head housing
46. Lobby
47. Boatswain's store room
48. Boatswain's store room
49. Sail room
50. Shot locker
51. Hold well
52. Spirit room
53. Fish room
54. Bread room
55. Mast step
56. Keelson
57. Ceilings

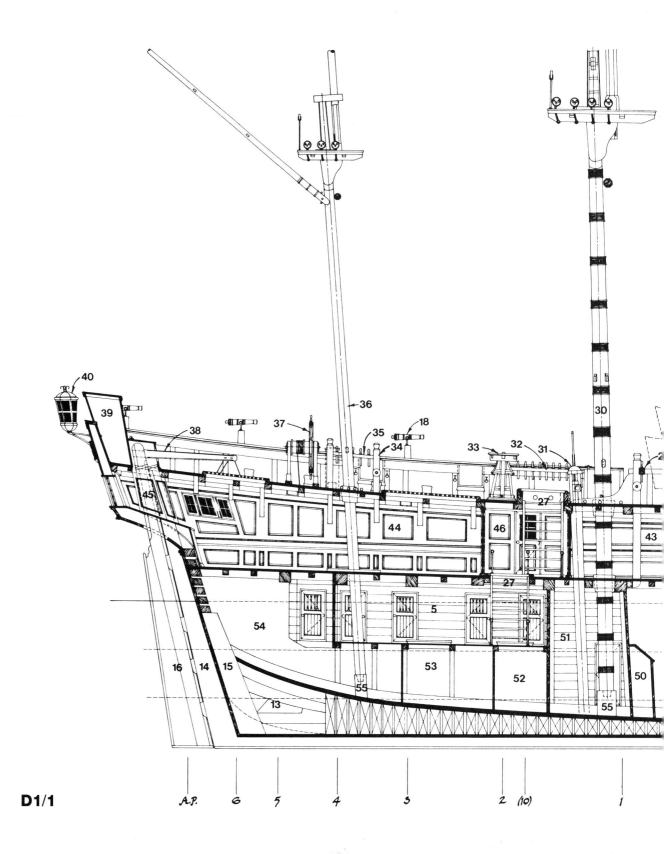

D1/1

A.P.   6   5   4   3   2 (10)   1

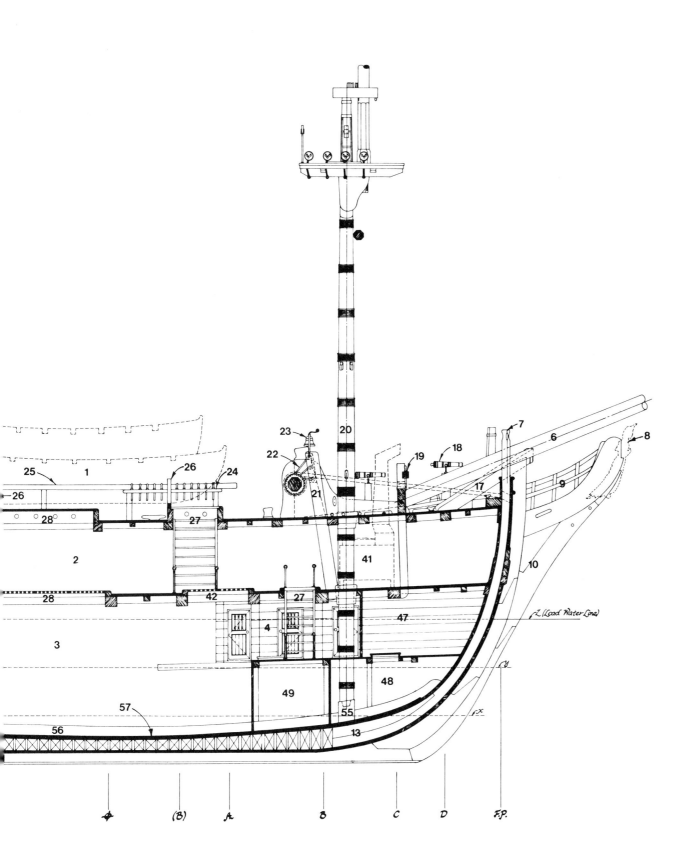

25 1

26

26 24

28

27

2

23

22 21

20

41

19 18

17

7

6

8

9

10

28 42

27 4 47

L (Load Water Line)

3

48

49 Y

55 X

57

56 13

D Internal hull

**D1/2 Inboard profile of *Bethia*
showing alterations (1/96 scale)**

1. Swivel guns and stanchions added
2. Flag locker added
3. Fore brace bitts altered
4. Great cabin renovated to form greenhouse
5. Deck locker removed; gratings installed
6. Ports added to hatch and companionway coamings
7. Gratings added aft of wheel
8. Companionway reduced
9. Carpenter's and Boatswain's cabins removed port and starboard
10. Scuttle and ladder removed
11. Pantry and Captain's dining cabin added
12. Stove and galley removed from hold
13. Galley stove chimney removed
14. New galley stove installed
15. Cabins rearranged at fore platform
16. Cabins rearranged at aft platform
17. Air scuttles added (three locations port and three locations starboard)
18. Shot locker added
19. Hold well (pump well) added
20. Changes to hold under fore platform
21. Changes to hold under aft platform
22. Timberhead at cathead modified
23. Belfry modified at windlass pawl bitt post
24. Bowsprit steeve changed
25. Masts restepped on mast steps
26. Boat chocks and boats added

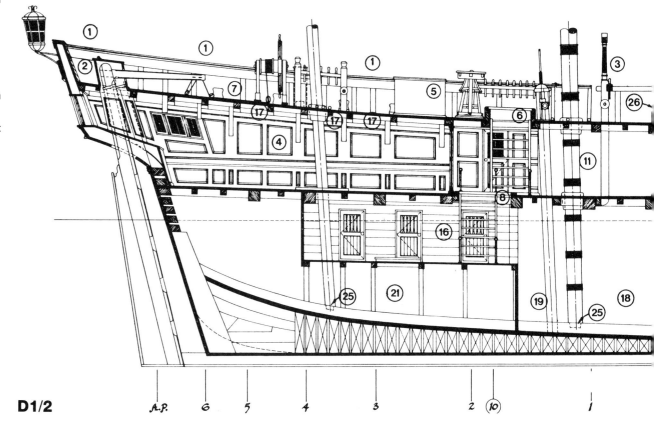

D1/2

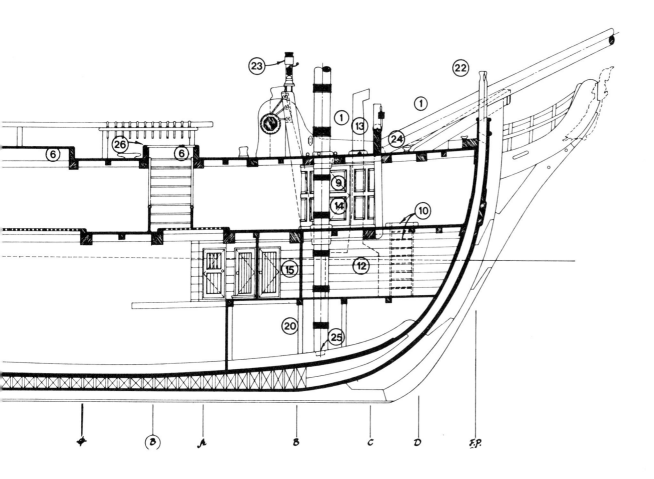

D Internal hull

D2 UPPER DECK

D2/1 Upper deck framing plan
(1/96 scale)
1. Cutwater
2. Open for scuttle
3. Open for galley chimney
4. Foremast
5. Open for companionway
6. Main hatch
7. Mainmast
8. Mizzen mast
9. Elm tree pump
10. Open for companionway
11. Carlings (support for capstan)
12. Open for gratings
13. Open for rudder
14. Deck clamp
15. Lodging knee
16. Deck beams – numbers correspond to adjacent frames
17. Hanging knees
18. Fore-and-aft carlings
19. Athwartship carlings (ledges)
20. Frames
21. Stern timber
22. Deck transom
23. Deck clamp

D2/2 Upper deck (1/96 scale)
1. Bowsprit
2. Head rails
3. Knighthead
4. Cathead
5. Breast hook
6. Bower anchor
7. Half-pounder swivel
8. Scuttle (with grating)
9. Galley stove chimney
10. Foremast
11. Pawl bitt post
12. Carrick bitts
13. Pawls and pawl rim
14. Fore channel
15. Fore pin rail
16. Rail
17. Chesstree
18. Companionway
19. Main hatch
20. Boat chock
21. Fore brace bitts
22. Side ladder
23. Mainmast
24. Elm tree pump
25. Main pin rail
26. Main channel
27. Capstan
28. 4-pounder gun (short)
29. Grating
30. Mizzen mast
31. Binnacle
32. Mizzen topsail sheet bitts
33. Steering wheel
34. Mizzen channel
35. Poop pin rail
36. Quarter gallery or badge light
37. Tiller
38. Rudder head housing
39. Flag locker
40. Stern lantern
41. Taffrail
42. Sheave (in bulwark)
43. Fore topsail sheet bitts

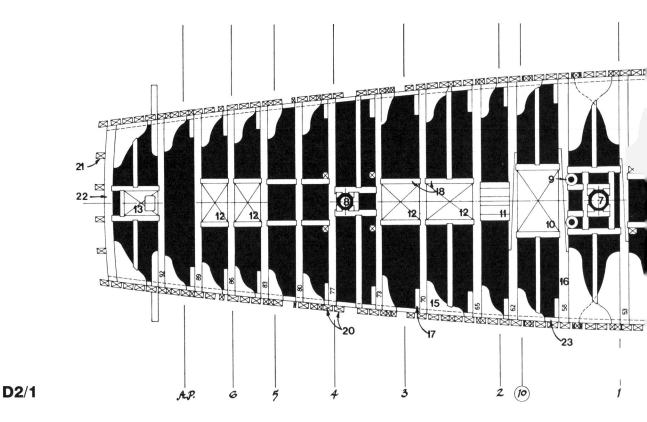

D2/1

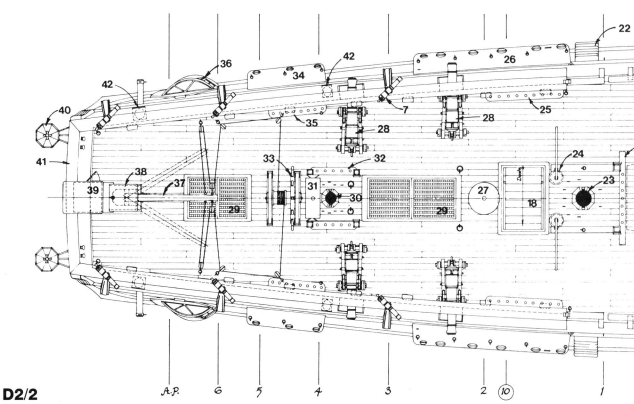

D2/2

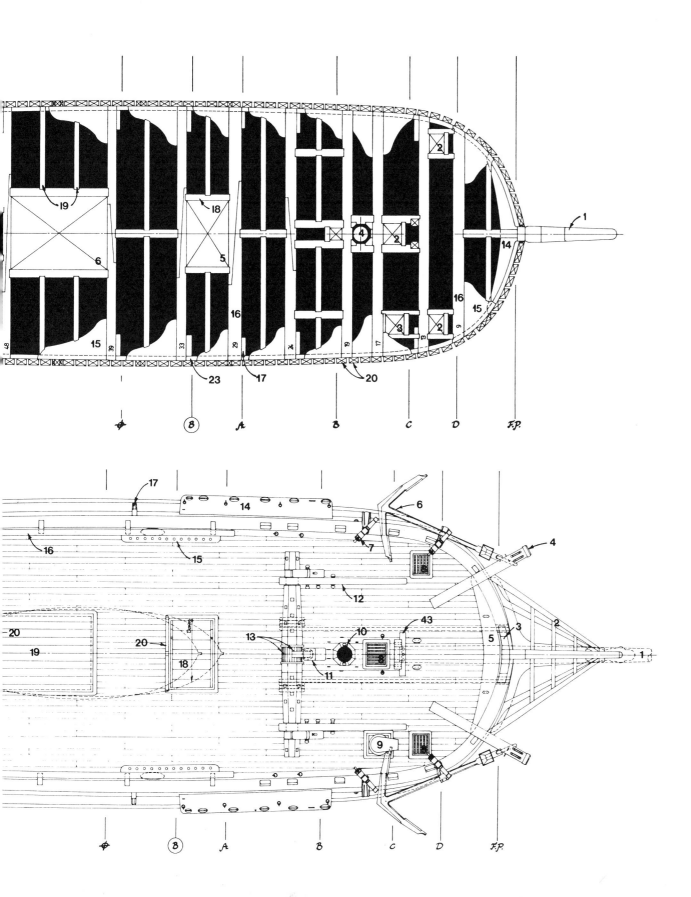

D Internal hull

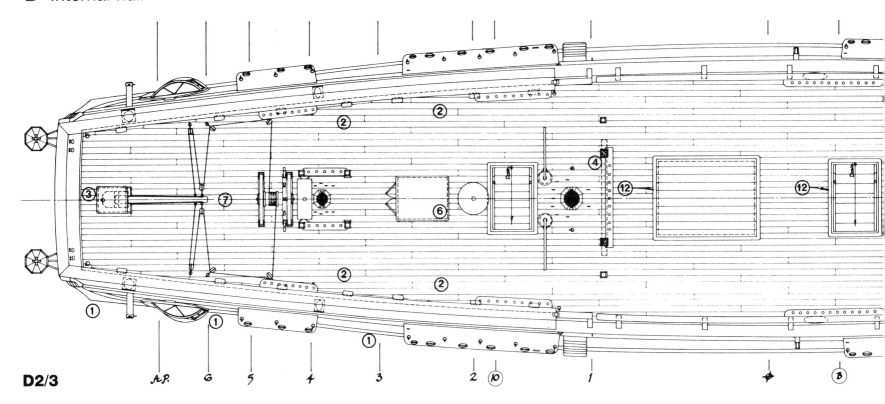

D2/3

A.P.   6   5   4   3   2 ⑩   1   ✦   ⑧

**D2/3 Upper deck plan of *Bethia*
showing alterations (1/96 scale)**

1. Swivel guns and stanchions added
   (five locations port and five locations
   starboard)
2. 4-pounder guns added and ports cut
   into bulwarks (two locations port and
   two locations starboard)
3. Flag locker added
4. Fore brace bitts altered
5. Air scuttles added to forecastle port
   and starboard
6. Deck locker removed; gratings
   installed
7. Gratings installed aft of wheel
8. Galley stove chimney removed
9. Galley stove chimney installed
10. Timberhead at cathead modified
11. Modifications to belfry at windlass
    pawl bitt
12. Boat chocks and boats added

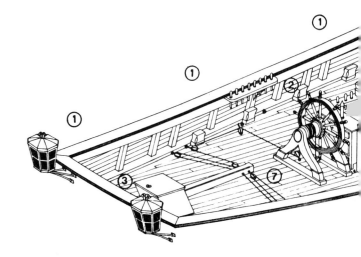

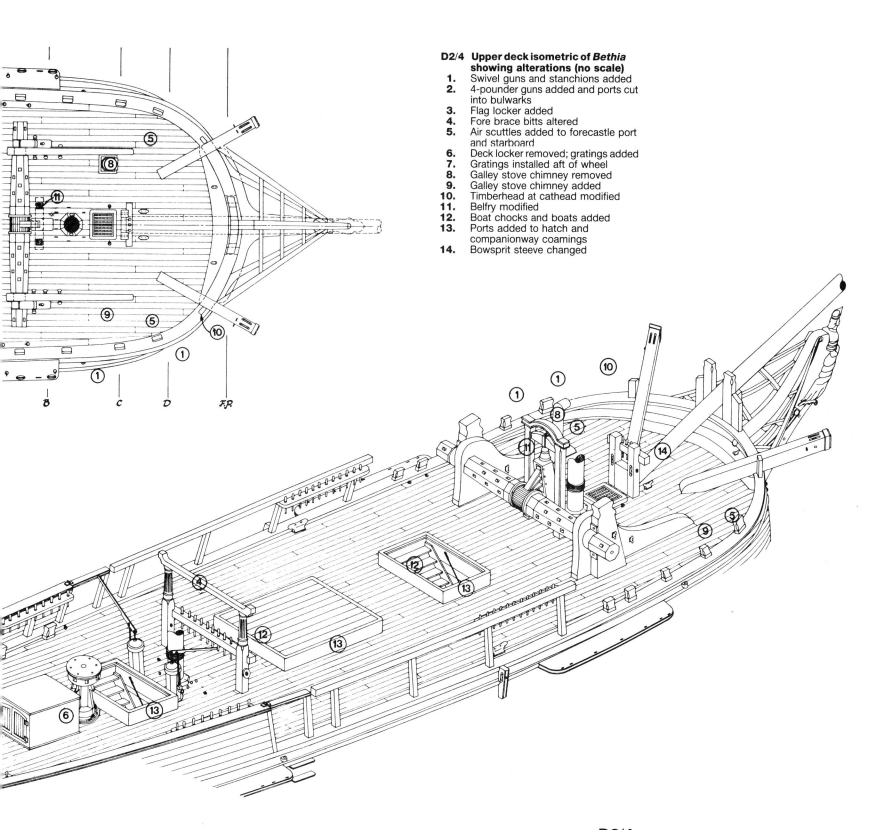

D2/4 Upper deck isometric of *Bethia* showing alterations (no scale)

1. Swivel guns and stanchions added
2. 4-pounder guns added and ports cut into bulwarks
3. Flag locker added
4. Fore brace bitts altered
5. Air scuttles added to forecastle port and starboard
6. Deck locker removed; gratings added
7. Gratings installed aft of wheel
8. Galley stove chimney removed
9. Galley stove chimney added
10. Timberhead at cathead modified
11. Belfry modified
12. Boat chocks and boats added
13. Ports added to hatch and companionway coamings
14. Bowsprit steeve changed

D2/4

D Internal hull

D3 LOWER DECK

D3/1 Lower deck framing plan (1/96 scale)

1. Cutwater
2. Foremast
3. Open for companionway
4. Fore hatch
5. Main hatch
6. Mainmast
7. Mizzen mast
8. Stern post
9. Lodging knee
10. Hanging knee
11. Deck beams – numbers correspond to adjacent frames
12. Transom knee
13. Transom
14. Counter timber
15. Stern timber
16. Fore-and-aft carlings
17. Athwartship carlings (ledges)
18. Frames
19. Deck clamp

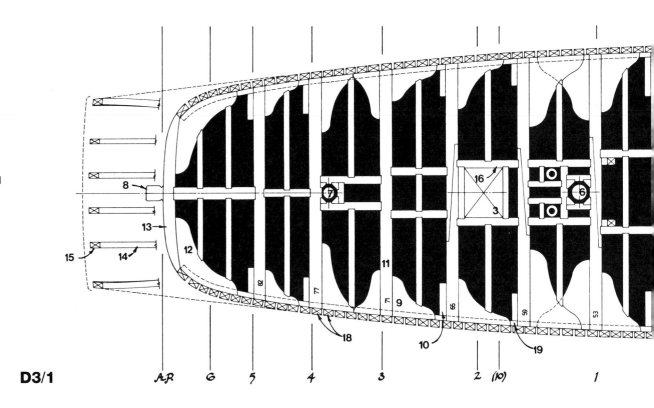

D3/1

D3/2 Lower deck (1/96 scale)

1. Cutwater
2. Pin of fore topsail sheet bitts
3. Galley stove
4. Foremast
5. Pawl bitt post
6. Companionway
7. Fore hatch
8. Main hatch
9. Pantry
10. Captain's dining cabin
11. Pin of fore brace bitts
12. Mainmast
13. Elm tree pump
14. Captain's cabin
15. Lobby
16. Master's cabin
17. Garden (great cabin)
18. Mizzen mast
19. Quarter gallery
20. Stern post
21. Rudder

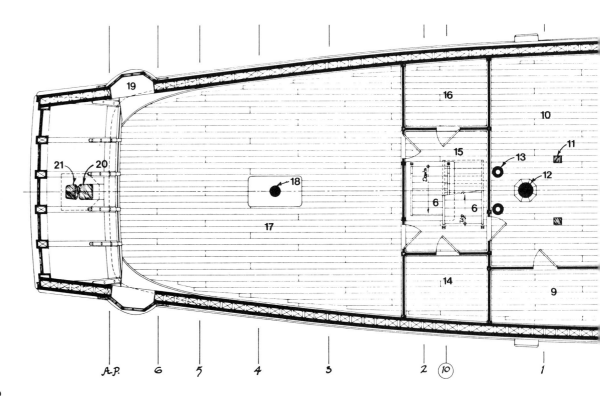

D3/2

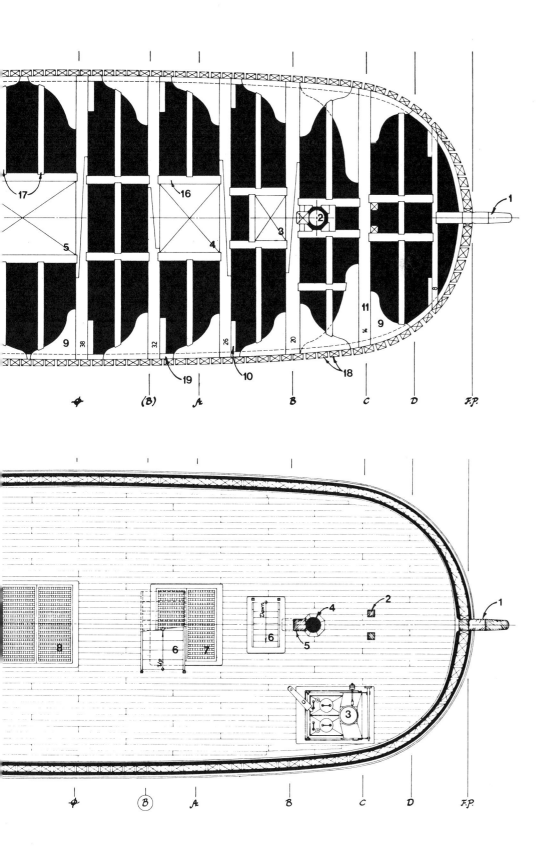

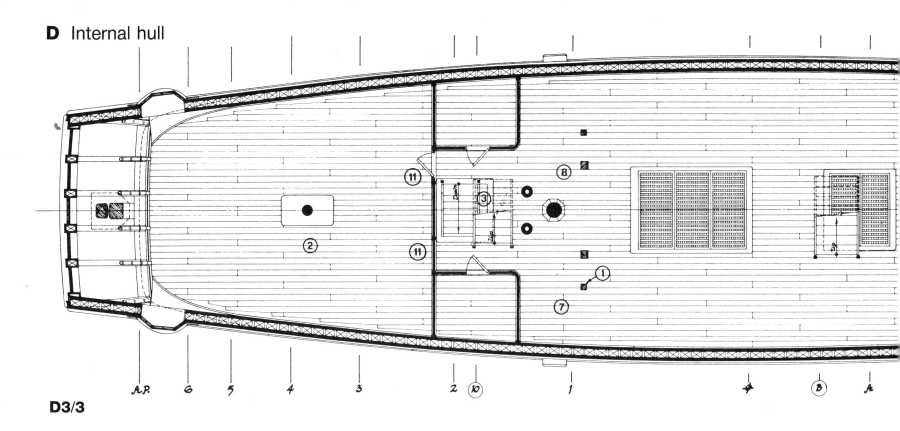

D3/3

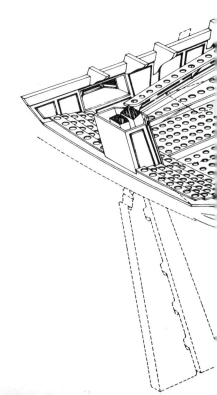

**D3/3 Lower deck plan of *Bethia*
showing alterations (1/96 scale)**

1. Fore brace bitts altered
2. Great cabin altered to form greenhouse
3. Aft companionway reduced
4. Boatswain's cabin removed
5. Carpenter's cabin removed
6. Scuttle (and ladder) to galley removed
7. Pantry added
8. Captain's dining room added
9. Galley stove chimney removed
10. Galley stove chimney installed
11. Doors changed to great cabin (gar-
    den)
12. Companionway to fore platform
    added

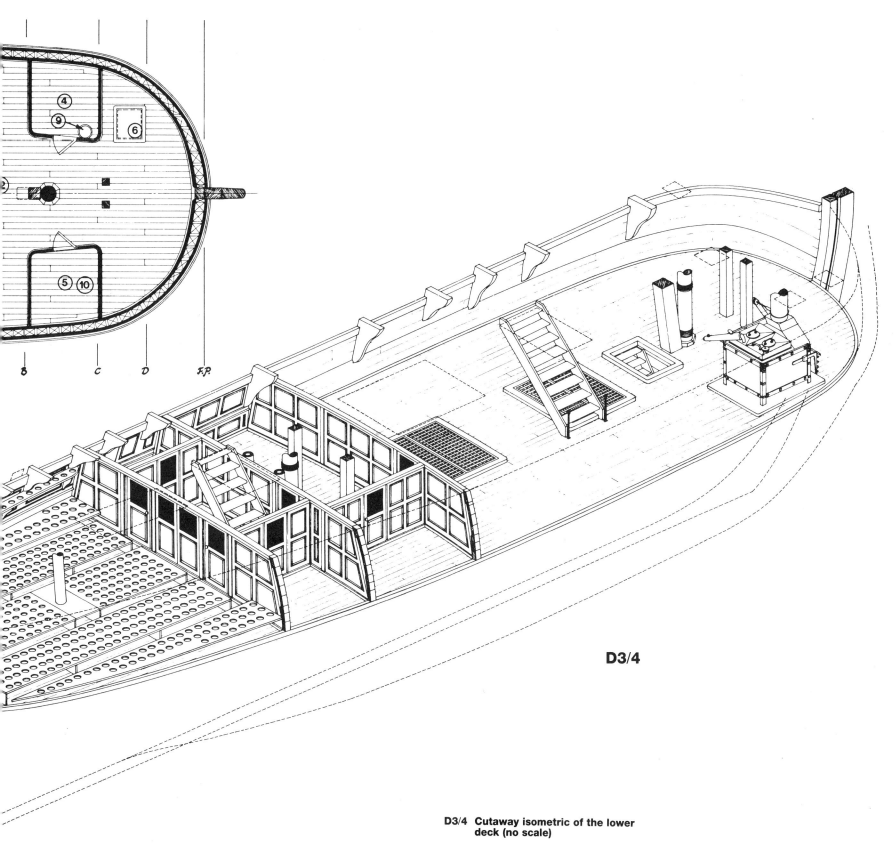

B   C   D   F.P.

D3/4

D3/4 Cutaway isometric of the lower deck (no scale)

D Internal hull

D4 HOLD

D4/1 Platform framing (1/96 scale)
1. Cutwater
2. Open for scuttles
3. Foremast
4. Mainmast
5. Mizzen mast
6. Beam (to support cabin over)
7. Carlings
8. Stern post
9. Beams (note pillars under)
10. Frames

D4/2 Hold (1/96 scale)
1. Cutwater
2. Carpenter's store room
3. Gunner's store room
4. Boatswain's store room
5. Sail room
6. Scuttle to magazine
7. Scuttle to Boatswain's stores
8. Carpenter's cabin
9. Fore platform
10. Boatswain's cabin
11. Pitch room
12. Block room
13. Companionway
14. Scuttle to sail room
15. Foremast
16. Hold
17. Fore hatch over
18. Main hatch over
19. Shot locker
20. Hold well or pump well
21. Mainmast
22. Elm tree pumps
23. Aft platform
24. Companionway
25. Scuttle to spirit room
26. Scuttle to fish room
27. Scuttle to magazine
28. Slop room
29. Captain's store room
30. Gunner's cabin
31. Botanist's cabin
32. Captain's clerk's cabin
33. Surgeon's cabin
34. Steward's room
35. Mizzen mast
36. Bread room
37. Stern post
38. Rudder

D4/1

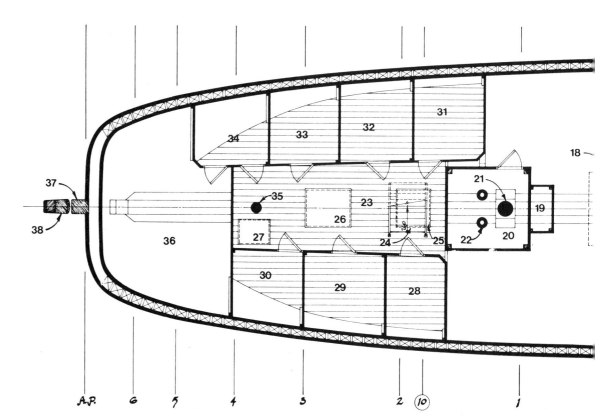

D4/2

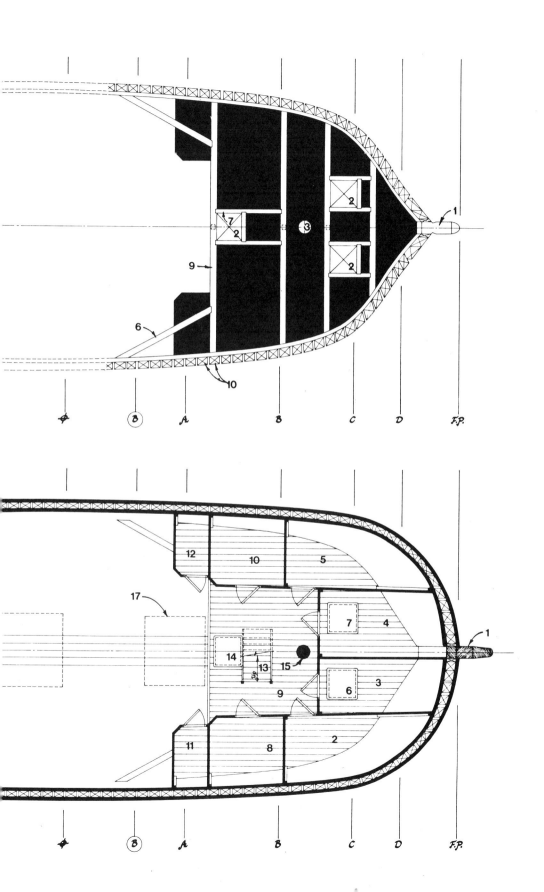

69

D Internal hull

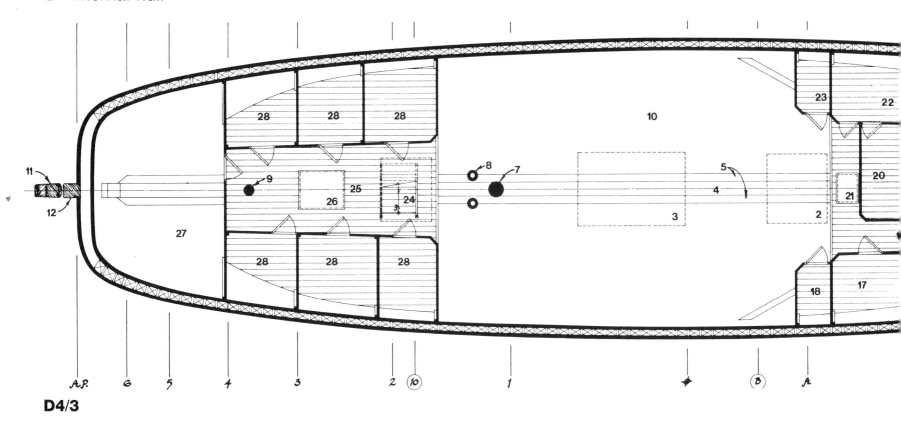

D4/3

D4/3 Hold plan of *Bethia* (1/96 scale)
1. Cutwater
2. Fore hatch over
3. Main hatch over
4. Keelson
5. Limber board
6. Foremast
7. Mainmast
8. Elm tree pumps
9. Mizzen mast
10. Hold
11. Rudder
12. Stern post
13. Sail room
14. Galley
15. Galley stove
16. Ladder (scuttle over)
17. Carpenter's store room
18. Pitch room
19. Passage
20. Sail room
21. Scuttle
22. Boatswain's store room
23. Block room
24. Companionway
25. Aft platform
26. Scuttle
27. Bread room
28. Cabins and store rooms

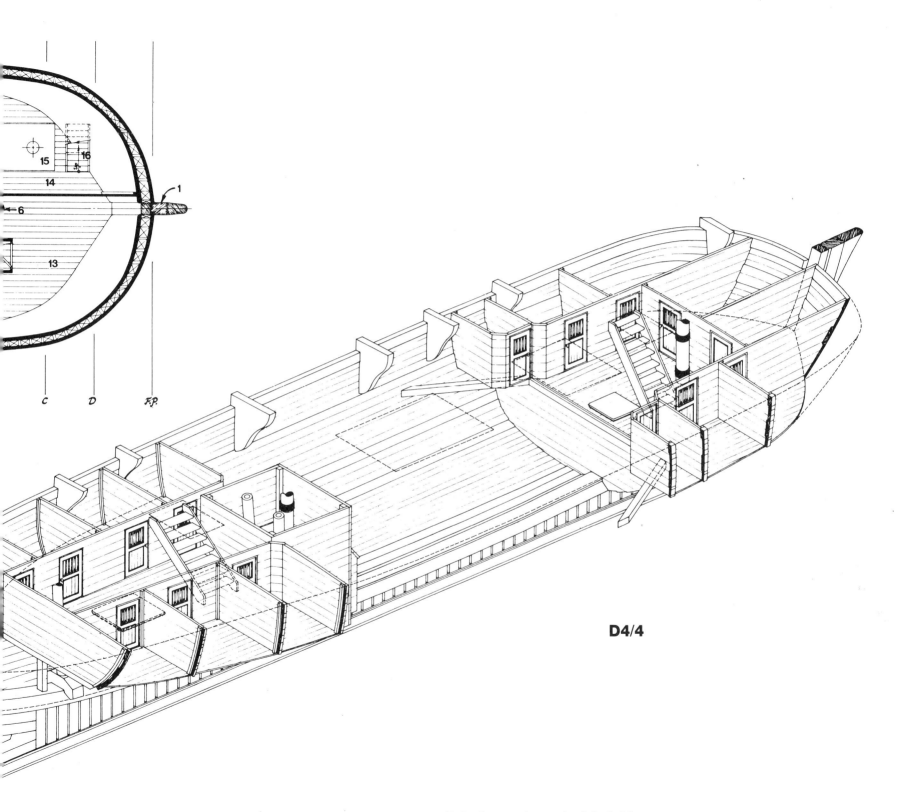

15

16

14

1

6

13

C   D   F.P.

D4/4

D4/4 Cutaway isometric of the hold
(no scale)

D Internal hull

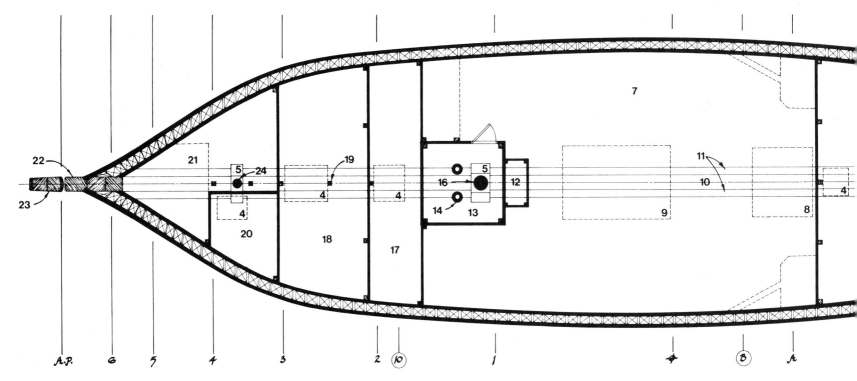

D4/5

D4/5 Hold (below palleting) (1/96 scale)
1. Cutwater
2. Forward magazine
3. Boatswain's store room
4. Scuttle over
5. Mast step
6. Sail room
7. Hold
8. Fore hatch over
9. Main hatch over
10. Keelson
11. Limber board
12. Shot locker
13. Hold well
14. Elm tree pumps
15. Foremast
16. Mainmast
17. Spirit room
18. Fish room
19. Pillar
20. Aft magazine
21. Bread room
22. Stern post
23. Rudder
24. Mizzen mast

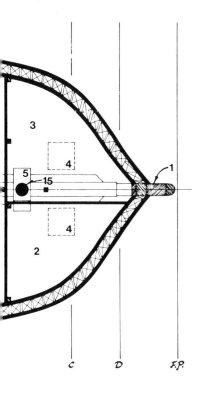

D5   STERN GARDEN

D5/1   Plan (1/96 scale)
1. Captain's cabin
2. Lobby
3. Master's cabin
4. Garden
5. Mizzen mast
6. Pot racks
7. Pot racks at ship's side
8. Quarter gallery

D5/2   Side elevation (1/96 scale)
1. Garden
2. Gratings
3. Line of mizzen mast
4. Pot racks

D5/3   Aft elevation (1/96 scale)

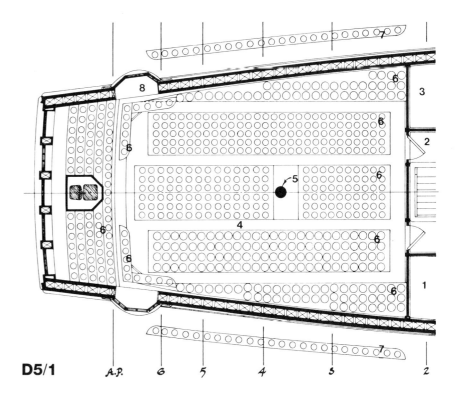

D5/1

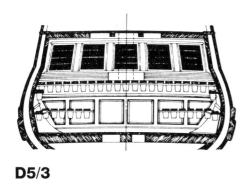

D5/3

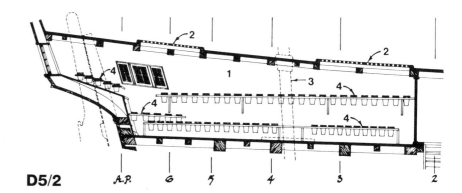

D5/2

D Internal hull

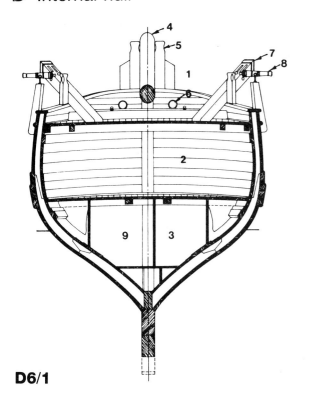

D6/1

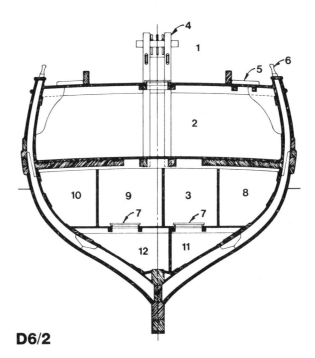

D6/2

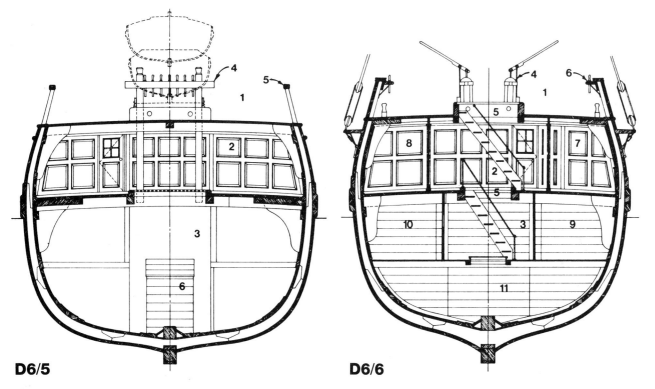

D6/5

D6/6

D6   CROSS SECTION

D6/1 Cross section at 'D' looking forward (1/96 scale)
1. Forecastle
2. Lower deck
3. Hold (Gunner's store room)
4. Bowsprit
5. Knighthead
6. Hawse hole
7. Cathead
8. Half-pounder swivel
9. Boatswain's store room

D6/2 Cross section at 'C' looking forward (1/96 scale)
1. Forecastle
2. Lower deck
3. Hold (Gunner's store room)
4. Fore topsail sheet bitts
5. Scuttle
6. Timberhead
7. Scuttle
8. Carpenter's store room
9. Boatswain's store room
10. Sail room
11. Magazine
12. Boatswain's store room

D6/5 Cross section at ⊕ looking aft (1/96 scale)
1. Upper deck
2. Lower deck
3. Hold
4. Fore brace bitts
5. Rail
6. Shot locker

D6/6 Cross section at ⑩ looking forward (1/96 scale)
1. Upper deck
2. Lower deck (lobby)
3. Hold
4. Elm tree pump
5. Companionway
6. Main pin rail
7. Captain's cabin
8. Master's cabin
9. Slop room
10. Botanist's cabin
11. Spirit room

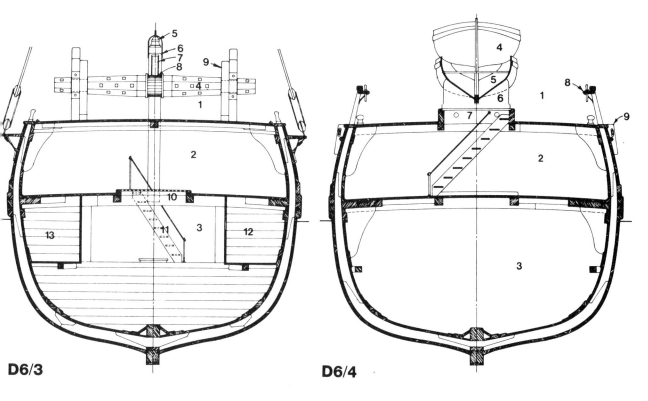

D6/3 Cross section at 'A' looking forward (1/96 scale)
1. Forecastle
2. Lower deck
3. Hold
4. Windlass
5. Bell
6. Pawl bitt post
7. Pawls
8. Pawl rim
9. Carrick bitt
10. Fore hatch
11. Companion
12. Pitch room
13. Block room

D6/4 Cross section at B looking aft (1/96 scale)
1. Upper deck
2. Lower deck
3. Hold
4. Cutter
5. Launch
6. Boat chock
7. Companionway
8. Fore pin rail
9. Chesstree

D6/3

D6/4

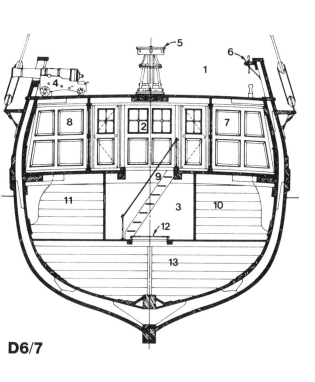

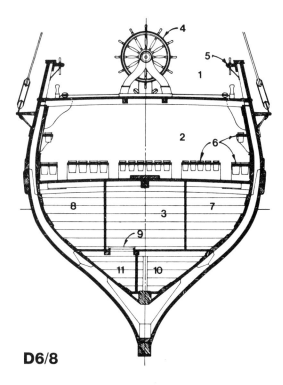

D6/7 Cross section at '2' looking aft (1/96 scale)
1. Upper deck
2. Lower deck (lobby)
3. Hold (aft platform)
4. 4-pounder gun (short)
5. Capstan
6. Main pin rail
7. Master's cabin
8. Captain's cabin
9. Companionway
10. Captain's clerk's cabin
11. Slop room
12. Scuttle
13. Spirit room

D6/8 Cross section at '4' looking aft (1/96 scale)
1. Quarterdeck
2. Lower deck (garden)
3. Hold (aft platform)
4. Steering wheel
5. Poop pin rail
6. Pot racks
7. Steward's room
8. Gunner's cabin
9. Scuttle
10. Bread room
11. After magazine

D6/7

D6/8

D6/9 Cross section at '5' looking aft (1/96 scale)

1. Quarterdeck
2. Lower deck (garden)
3. Hold (bread room)
4. Half-pounder swivel
5. Pot racks

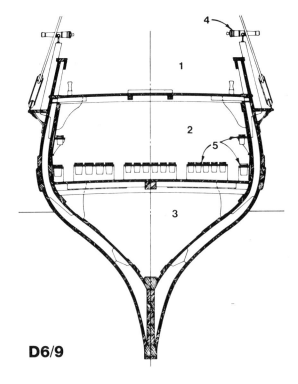

D6/9

D6/10 Cross section at '6' looking aft (1/96 scale)

1. Quarterdeck
2. Lower deck (garden)
3. Hold (bread room)
4. Half-pounder swivel
5. Quarter gallery
6. Stern lantern
7. Flag locker
8. Tiller
9. Grating

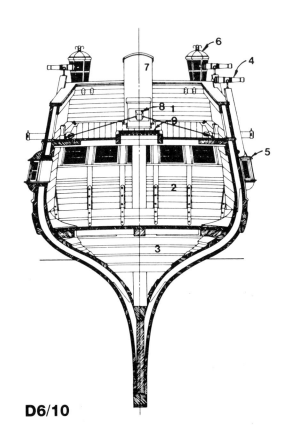

D6/10

E Fittings

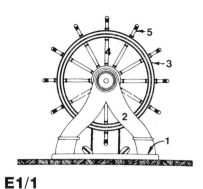

E1/1

E1/2

E1   STEERING GEAR

E1/1 Front elevation (1/48 scale)
1. Platform
2. Pedestal
3. Wheel rim
4. Spoke
5. Handle

E1/2 Side elevation (1/48 scale)
1. Wheel rim
2. Handle
3. Barrel
4. Pedestal
5. Platform
6. Tiller ropes

E1/3 Plan of gudgeon (1/32 scale)
1. Gudgeon
2. Stern post

E1/4 Plan of pintle (1/32 scale)
1. Pintle
2. Rudder

E1/5 Elevation of pintle and gudgeon (1/32 scale)
1. Stern post
2. Gudgeon
3. Rudder
4. Pintle

E1/6 Plan of spectacle plate

E1/7 Elevation of spectacle plate

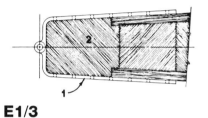

E1/3

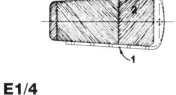

E1/4

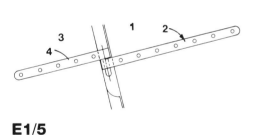

E1/5

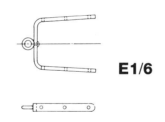

E1/6

E1/7

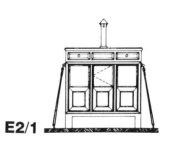

E2/1

E2/2

E2   BINNACLE

E2/1 Front elevation (1/48 scale)

E2/2 Side elevation (1/48 scale)

E2/3 Isometric view (no scale)

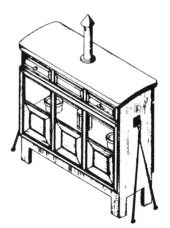

E2/3

E Fittings

E3/1   Sketch of quarter deck looking forward — tiller, wheel and binnacle (no scale)

E3/1

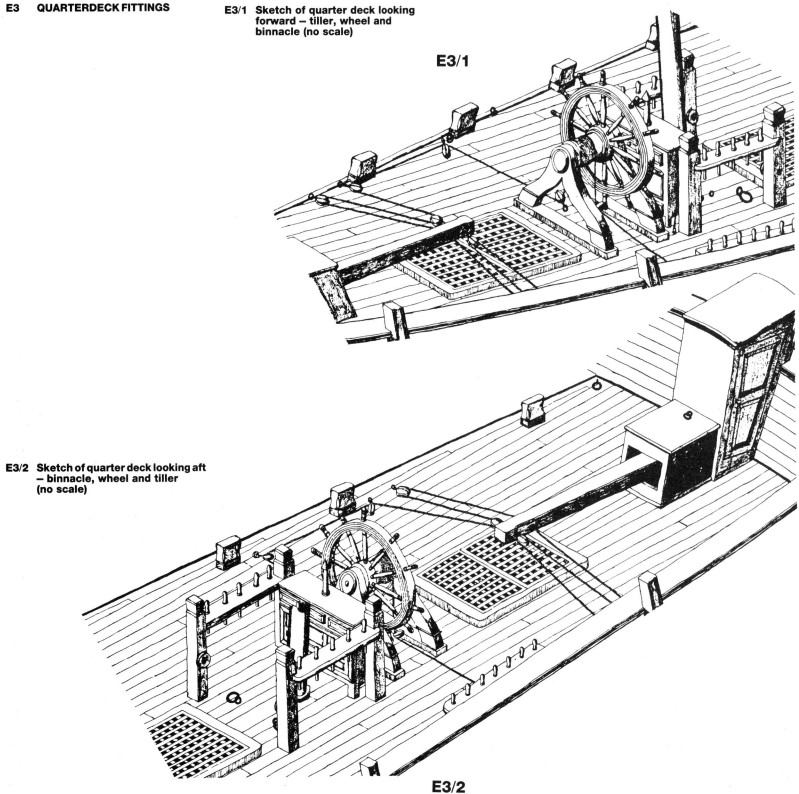

E3/2   Sketch of quarter deck looking aft — binnacle, wheel and tiller (no scale)

E3/2

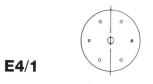

E4/1

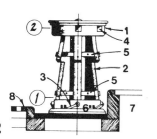

E4/2

Detail 2

Detail 1 **E4/3**

E4   **CAPSTAN**

E4/1   **Plan (1/48 scale)**

E4/2   **Side elevation (1/48 scale)**
   1.   Drumhead
   2.   Whelp
   3.   Pawl
   4.   Holes for bars
   5.   Chock
   6.   Plinth
   7.   Companionway
   8.   Grating

E4/3   **Details (1/48 scale)**

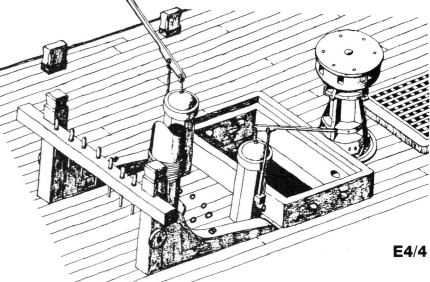

E4/4

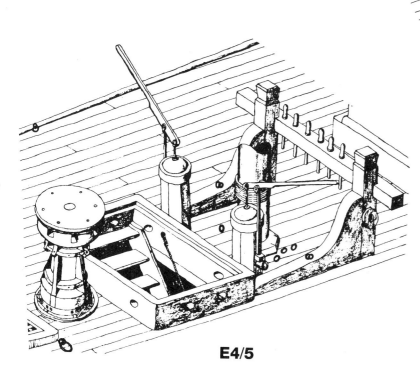

E4/5

E4/4   **Sketch of upper deck – fore brace bitts, pumps and capstan (no scale)**

E4/5   **Sketch of upper deck looking forward – capstan, pumps and fore brace bitts (no scale)**

E Fittings

E5 **LANTERN**

E5/1 **Plan (1/32 scale)**

E5/2 **Rear elevation (1/32 scale)**

E5/3 **Side elevation (1/32 scale)**

E5/4 **Isometric view (no scale)**

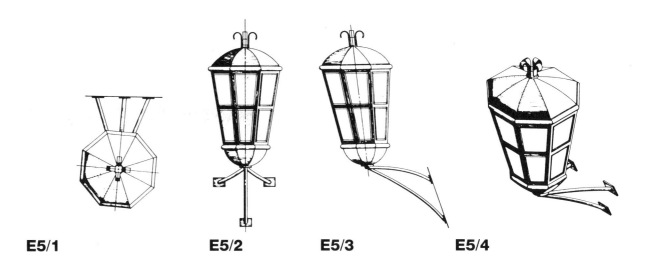

E5/1 **E5/2** **E5/3** **E5/4**

E6 **WINDLASS**

E6/1 **Sketch of forecastle looking aft –
windlass (no scale)**

E6/2 **Sketch of forecastle looking
forward – windlass (no scale)**

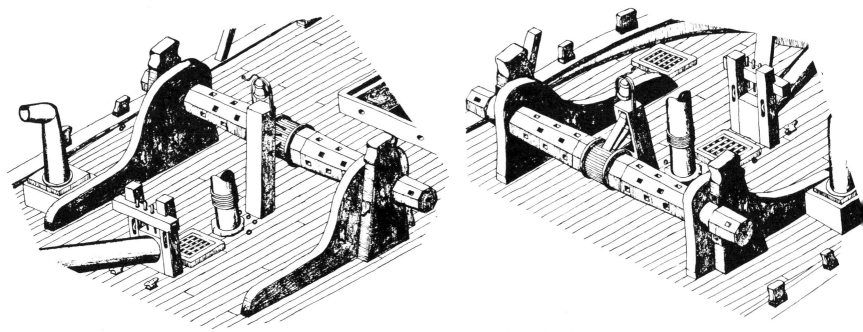

E6/1 **E6/2**

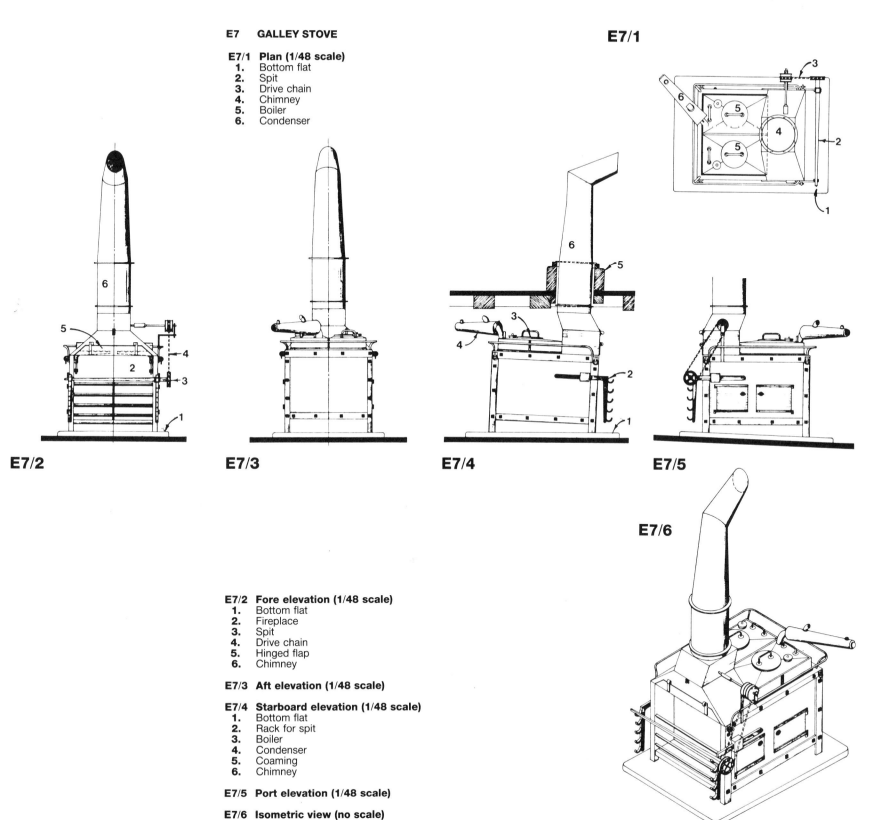

E7 GALLEY STOVE

E7/1 Plan (1/48 scale)
1. Bottom flat
2. Spit
3. Drive chain
4. Chimney
5. Boiler
6. Condenser

E7/1

E7/2

E7/3

E7/4

E7/5

E7/6

E7/2 Fore elevation (1/48 scale)
1. Bottom flat
2. Fireplace
3. Spit
4. Drive chain
5. Hinged flap
6. Chimney

E7/3 Aft elevation (1/48 scale)

E7/4 Starboard elevation (1/48 scale)
1. Bottom flat
2. Rack for spit
3. Boiler
4. Condenser
5. Coaming
6. Chimney

E7/5 Port elevation (1/48 scale)

E7/6 Isometric view (no scale)

E Fittings

E8 ANCHORS

E8/1 Bower anchor: plan (1/96 scale)
1. Ring
2. Square
3. Nut (within)
4. Stock
5. Hoop

E8/2 Bower anchor: side elevation (1/96 scale)
1. Ring
2. Square
3. Stock
4. Shank
5. Palm
6. Bill shape
7. Blade
8. Arm
9. Crown
10. Small

E8/3 Bower anchor: front elevation (1/96 scale)
1. Ring
2. Square
3. Stock
4. Shank
5. Palm
6. Arm
7. Nut (within)
8. Hoop
9. Small

E8/4 Stream anchor: side elevation (1/96 scale)
1. Ring
2. Square
3. Eye
4. Small
5. Shank
6. Palm
7. Bill shape
8. Blade
9. Arm
10. Crown

E8/5 Stream anchor: front elevation (1/96 scale)
1. Ring
2. Square
3. Ironstock
4. Ring forelock
5. Small
6. Shank
7. Palm
8. Arm

E8/6 Kedge anchor: side elevation (1/96 scale)

E8/7 Kedge anchor: front elevation (1/96 scale)

E8/1

E8/2

E8/3

E8/4

E8/5

E8/6

E8/7

F Armament

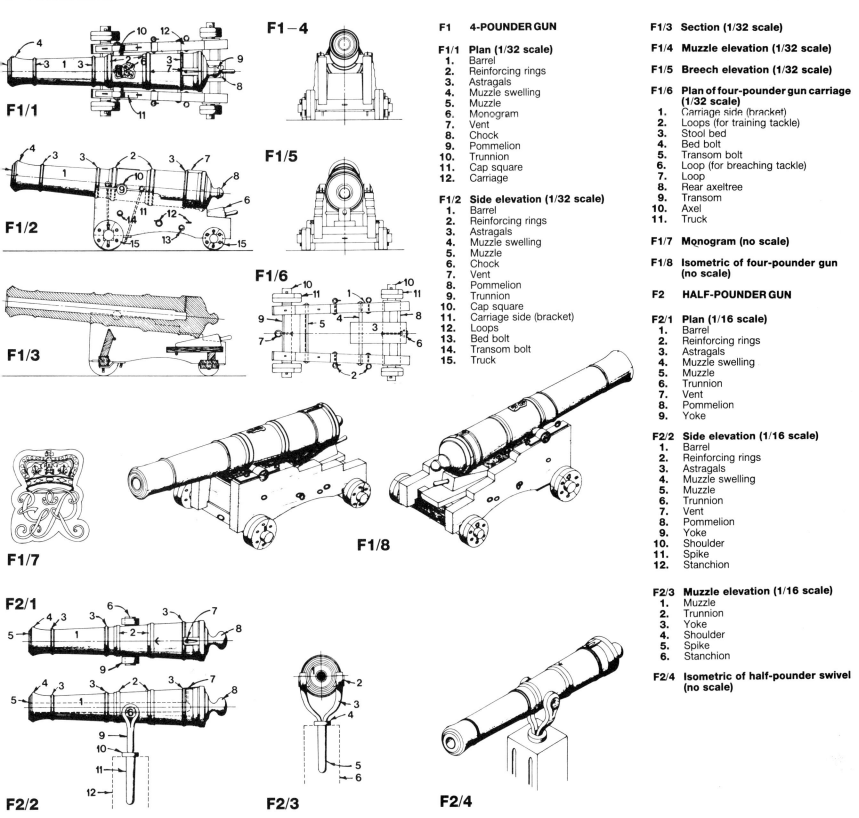

F1/1

F1/2

F1/3

F1/7

F1–4

F1/5

F1/6

F1/8

F2/1

F2/2

F2/3

F2/4

F1   **4-POUNDER GUN**

F1/1   **Plan (1/32 scale)**
1. Barrel
2. Reinforcing rings
3. Astragals
4. Muzzle swelling
5. Muzzle
6. Monogram
7. Vent
8. Chock
9. Pommelion
10. Trunnion
11. Cap square
12. Carriage

F1/2   **Side elevation (1/32 scale)**
1. Barrel
2. Reinforcing rings
3. Astragals
4. Muzzle swelling
5. Muzzle
6. Chock
7. Vent
8. Pommelion
9. Trunnion
10. Cap square
11. Carriage side (bracket)
12. Loops
13. Bed bolt
14. Transom bolt
15. Truck

F1/3   **Section (1/32 scale)**

F1/4   **Muzzle elevation (1/32 scale)**

F1/5   **Breech elevation (1/32 scale)**

F1/6   **Plan of four-pounder gun carriage (1/32 scale)**
1. Carriage side (bracket)
2. Loops (for training tackle)
3. Stool bed
4. Bed bolt
5. Transom bolt
6. Loop (for breaching tackle)
7. Loop
8. Rear axeltree
9. Transom
10. Axel
11. Truck

F1/7   **Monogram (no scale)**

F1/8   **Isometric of four-pounder gun (no scale)**

F2   **HALF-POUNDER GUN**

F2/1   **Plan (1/16 scale)**
1. Barrel
2. Reinforcing rings
3. Astragals
4. Muzzle swelling
5. Muzzle
6. Trunnion
7. Vent
8. Pommelion
9. Yoke

F2/2   **Side elevation (1/16 scale)**
1. Barrel
2. Reinforcing rings
3. Astragals
4. Muzzle swelling
5. Muzzle
6. Trunnion
7. Vent
8. Pommelion
9. Yoke
10. Shoulder
11. Spike
12. Stanchion

F2/3   **Muzzle elevation (1/16 scale)**
1. Muzzle
2. Trunnion
3. Yoke
4. Shoulder
5. Spike
6. Stanchion

F2/4   **Isometric of half-pounder swivel (no scale)**

G Masts and spars

G1 **GENERAL ARRANGEMENTS**

G1/1 Isometric showing masts and
yards in position (no scale)

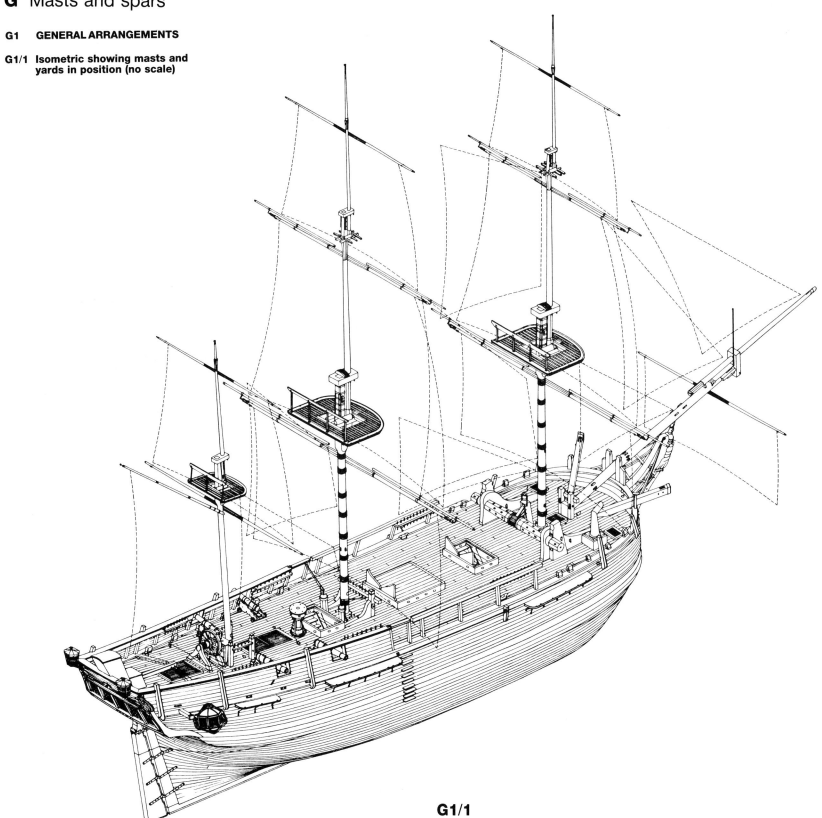

G1/1

G2 BOWSPRIT

G2/1 Plan (1/96 scale)

G2/2 Elevation (1/96 scale)

G2/3 Bowsprit (1/96 scale)

G2/4 Jibboom (1/96 scale)

G2/5 Spritsail yard (1/96 scale)

G2/6 Fish davit – plan and elevation (1/96 scale)

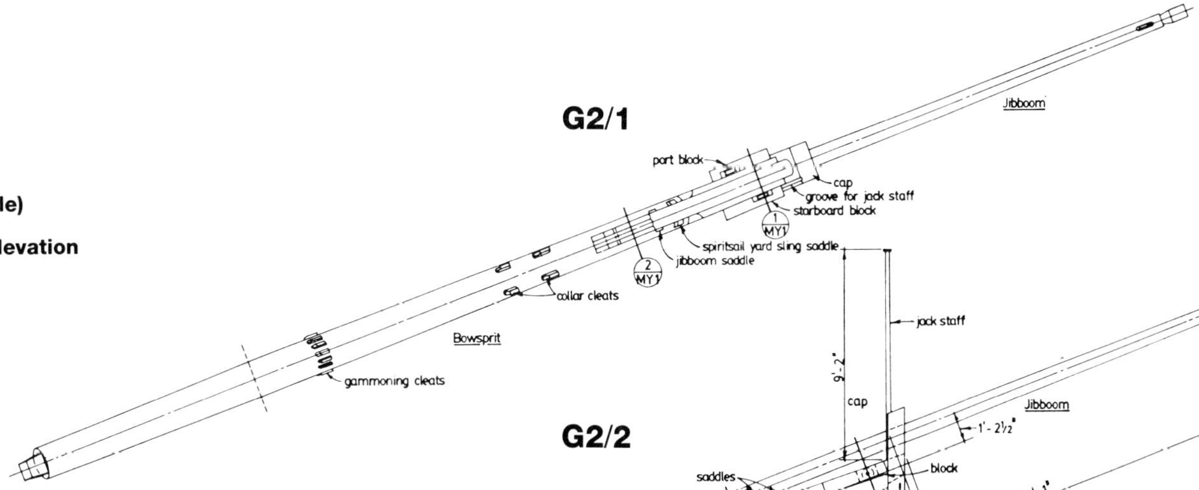

Jibboom
port block
cap
groove for jack staff
starboard block
spritsail yard sling saddle
jibboom saddle
collar cleats
Bowsprit
gammoning cleats

G2/1

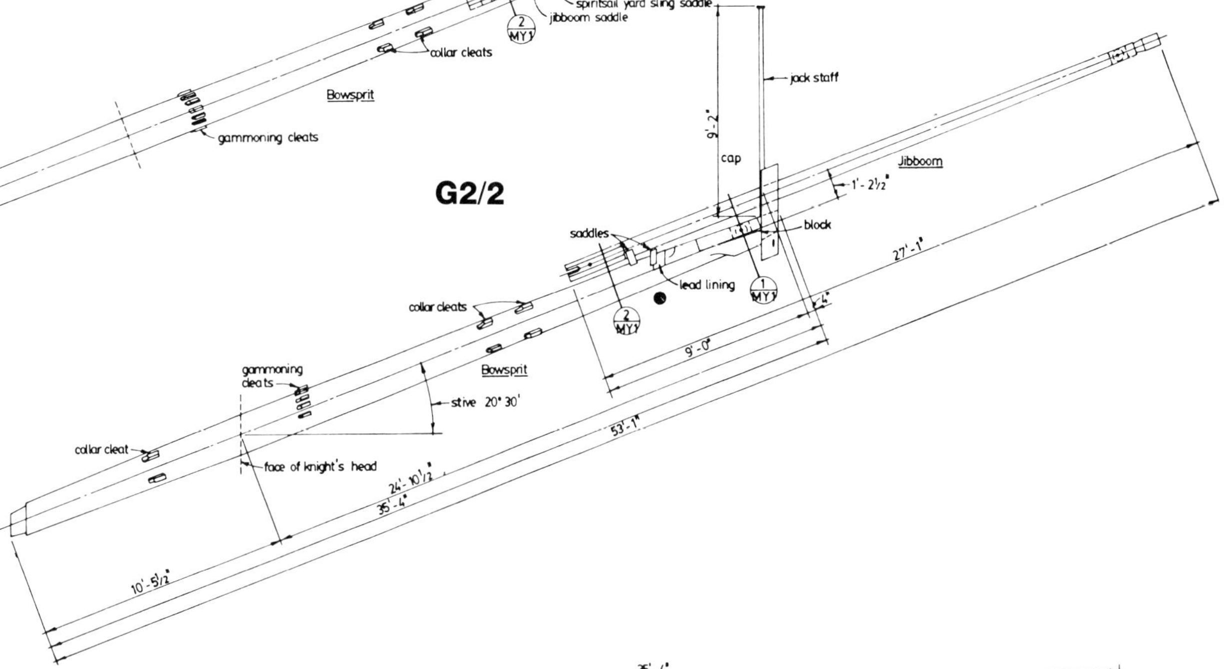

jack staff
9'-2"
cap
Jibboom
1'-2 1/2"
block
saddles
lead lining
27'-1"
4"
collar cleats
9'-0"
Bowsprit
gammoning cleats
stive 20° 30'
collar cleat
face of knight's head
53'-1"
24'-10 1/2"
35'-4"
10'-5 1/2"

G2/2

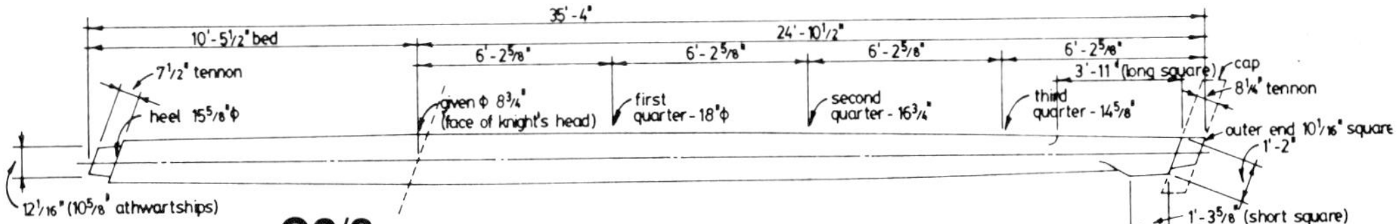

35'-4"
10'-5 1/2" bed
24'-10 1/2"
6'-2 5/8"
6'-2 5/8"
6'-2 5/8"
6'-2 5/8"
3'-11" (long square)
cap
7 1/2" tennon
8 1/4" tennon
heel 15 5/8"φ
given φ 8 3/4" (face of knight's head)
first quarter - 18"φ
second quarter - 16 3/4"
third quarter - 14 5/8"
outer end 10 1/16" square
1'-2"
12 1/16" (10 5/8" athwartships)
1'-3 5/8" (short square)

G2/3

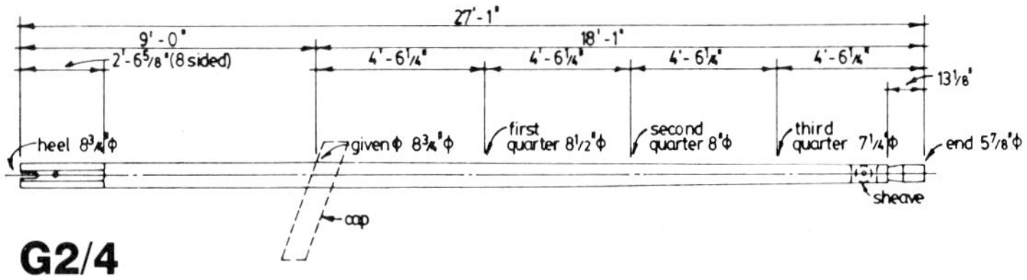

27'-1"
9'-0"
18'-1"
2'-6 5/8" (8 sided)
4'-6 1/4"
4'-6 1/4"
4'-6 1/4"
4'-6 1/4"
13 1/8"
heel 8 3/4"φ
given φ 8 3/4"φ
first quarter 8 1/2"φ
second quarter 8"φ
third quarter 7 1/4"φ
end 5 7/8"φ
sheave
cap

G2/4

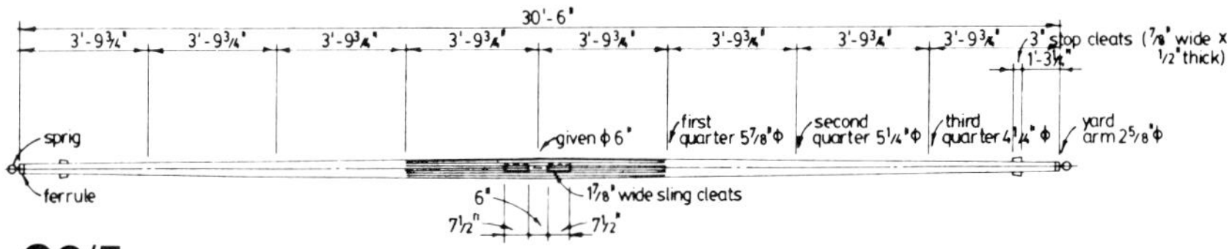

30'-6"
3'-9 3/4"
3'-9 3/4"
3'-9 3/4"
3'-9 3/4"
3'-9 3/4"
3'-9 3/4"
3'-9 3/4"
3'-9 3/4"
3" stop cleats (7/8" wide x 1/2" thick)
1'-3 1/4"
sprig
given φ 6"
first quarter 5 7/8"φ
second quarter 5 1/4"φ
third quarter 4 1/4"φ
yard arm 2 5/8"φ
ferrule
6"
1 7/8" wide sling cleats
7 1/2"
7 1/2"

G2/5

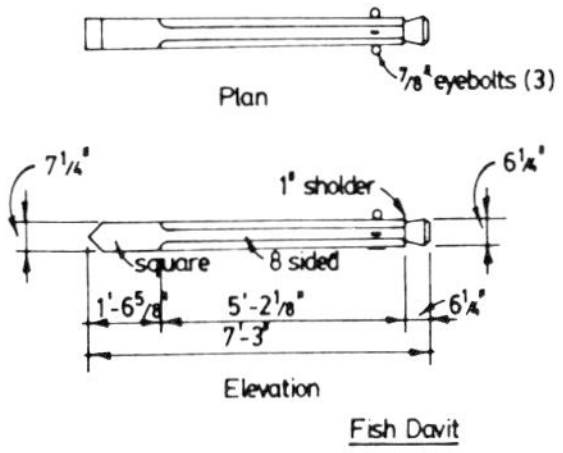

7/8" eyebolts (3)
Plan
7 1/4"
1" sholder
6 1/4"
square
8 sided
1'-6 5/8"
5'-2 1/8"
6 1/4"
7'-3"
Elevation
Fish Davit

G2/6

G Masts and spars

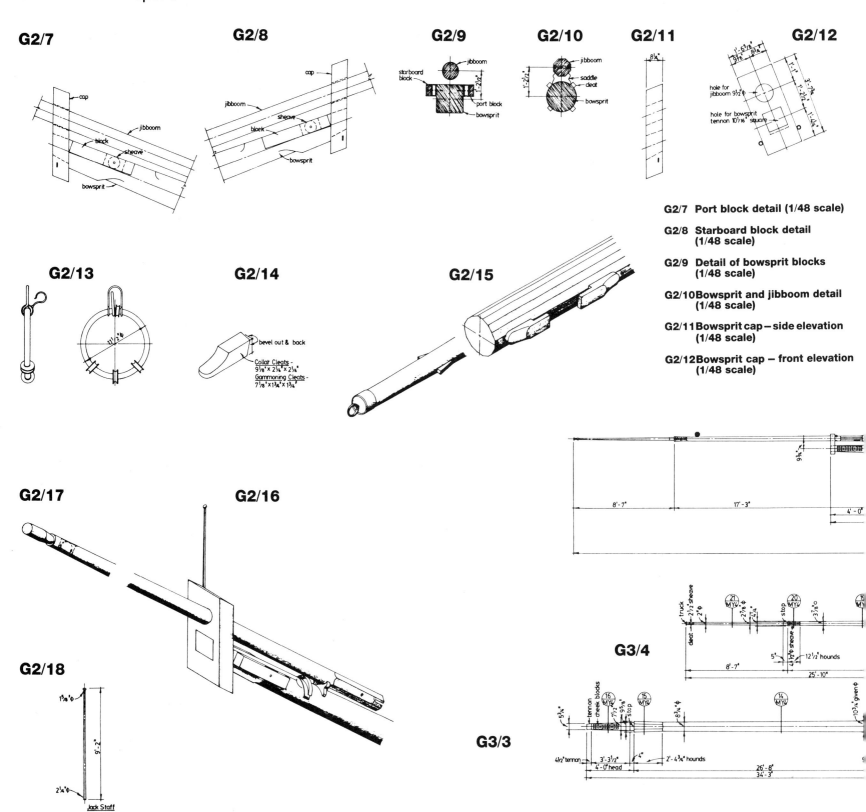

G2/7

G2/8

cap
jibboom
sheave
block
bowsprit

cap
jibboom
sheave
block
bowsprit

G2/9

starboard block
jibboom
port block
bowsprit

G2/10

jibboom
saddle
cleat
bowsprit

G2/11

8¼"

G2/12

1'-6⅝"
3½" 8¾"
1'-1" 3-7/16" 1'-2½" 1'-1¼"
hole for jibboom 9½"ø
hole for bowsprit tennon 10¹/₁₆" square

G2/7 Port block detail (1/48 scale)

G2/8 Starboard block detail (1/48 scale)

G2/9 Detail of bowsprit blocks (1/48 scale)

G2/10 Bowsprit and jibboom detail (1/48 scale)

G2/11 Bowsprit cap — side elevation (1/48 scale)

G2/12 Bowsprit cap — front elevation (1/48 scale)

G2/13

11½"ø

G2/14

bevel out & back
Collar Cleats - 9⅛" x 2¼" x 2¼"
Gammoning Cleats - 7⅛" x 1¾" x 1¾"

G2/15

G2/17

G2/16

G2/18

1⅝"ø
9'-2"
2¼"ø
Jack Staff

8'-7" 17'-3" 4'-0" 9¾"

G3/4

truck 2½" Sheave
cleat 2"ø
21 MY¼ 2⅞"ø 2¼"
stop 20 MY¼ 3⅞"ø
4½"ø sheave
5" 12½" hounds
8'-7"
25'-10"

tennon 5¾"
cheek blocks
16 MY¼ 7½" 9⅝"ø
stop 15 MY¼ 8¾"ø
14 MY¼ 10¾" given ø
4½" tennon 3'-3½" 4" 2'-4¾" hounds
4'-0" head
26'-8"
34'-3"

G3/3

86

G2/13 Jib traveller – front and side elevation (1/96 scale)

G2/14 Collar and gammoning cleats (no scale)

G2/15 Sketch of spritsail yard (no scale)

G2/16 Sketch of bowsprit (no scale)

G2/17 Sketch of jibboom end (no scale)

G2/18 Jack staff (1/96 scale)

G3   FOREMAST

G3/1 Foremast assembly (1/96 scale)

G3/2 Fore lower mast – front and side elevation (1/96 scale)

G3/3 Fore topmast (1/96 scale)

G3/4 Fore topgallant and pole mast (1/96 scale)

G4   FORE YARDS

G4/1 Fore yard (1/96 scale)

G4/2 Fore topmast yard (1/96 scale)

G4/1

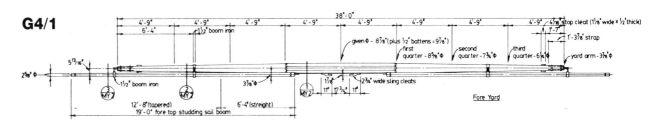

G4/2

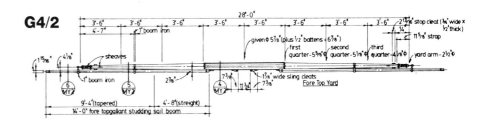

G3/1

G3/2

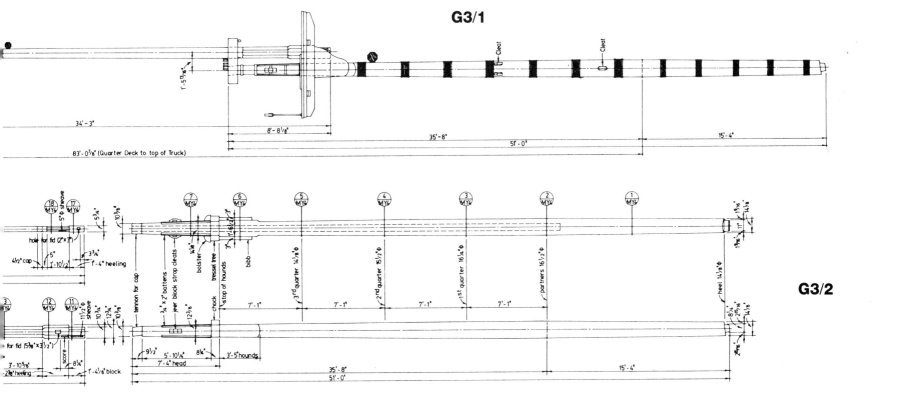

87

G Masts and spars

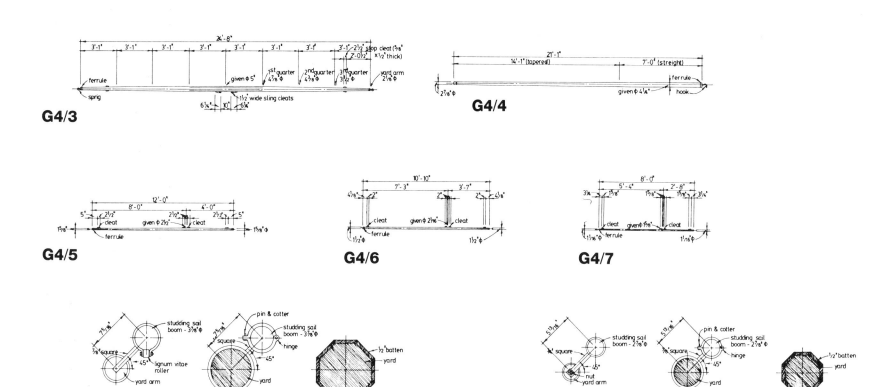

G4/3

G4/4

G4/5

G4/6

G4/7

G4/8

G4/9

G4/3 Fore topgallant yard (1/96 scale)

**G4/4 Fore lower studding sail boom
(1/96 scale)**

**G4/5 Fore studding sail yard
(1/96 scale)**

**G4/6 Fore top studding sail yard
(1/96 scale)**

**G4/7 Fore topgallant studding sail yard
(1/96 scale)**

G4/8 Fore yard details (1/16 scale)
1. Fore yard
2. Fore yard quarter iron
3. Fore yard studding sail boom iron

G4/9 Fore topyard details (1/16 scale)
4. Fore topyard
5. Fore topyard quarter iron
6. Fore topyard studding sail boom iron

G5 FORE TOPS

G5/1 Plan of fore top trees (1/96 scale)

G5/2 Plan of fore top (1/96 scale)

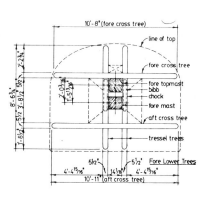

G5/1

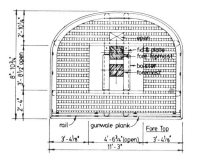

G5/2

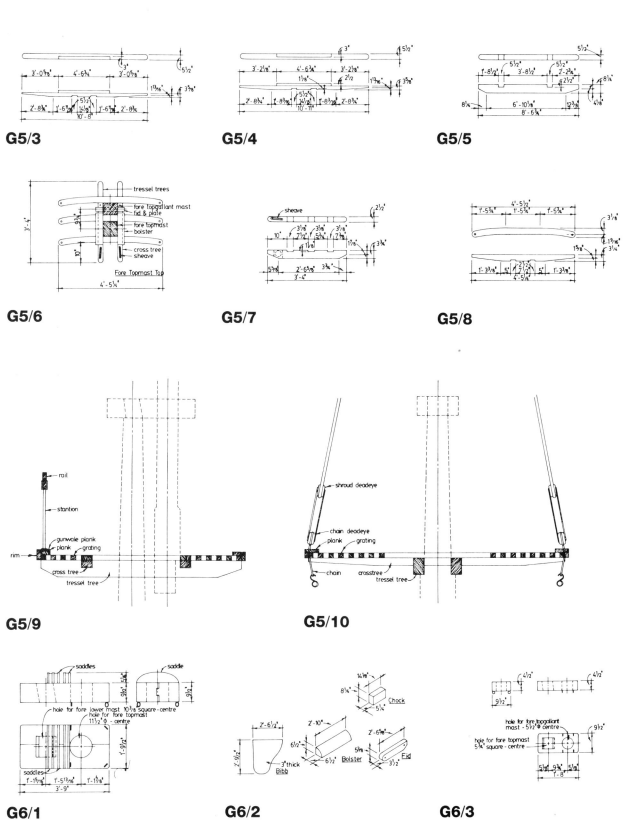

G5/3

G5/4

G5/5

G5/6

G5/7

G5/8

G5/9

G5/10

G6/1

G6/2

G6/3

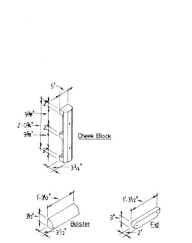

G6/4

G5/3 Plan and elevation of fore lower cross tree (forward) (1/96 scale)

G5/4 Plan and elevation of fore lower cross tree (aft) (1/96 scale)

G5/5 Plan and elevation of fore lower tressel trees (1/96 scale)

G5/6 Plan of fore topmast top (1/48 scale)

G5/7 Plan and elevation of fore top tressel trees (1/48 scale)

G5/8 Plan and elevation of fore top cross trees (1/48 scale)

G5/9 Section of fore top (fore and aft) (1/48 scale)

G5/10 Section of fore top (athwartships) (1/48 scale)

G6 FOREMAST DETAILS

G6/1 Fore lower mast cap – plan, side elevation and front elevation (1/48 scale)

G6/2 Fore lower mast – fid, bolster, chock and bibb (1/48 scale)

G6/3 Fore topmast cap – plan, side elevation and front elevation (1/48 scale)

G6/4 Fore topmast – fid, bolster and cheek block (1/48 scale)

G Masts and spars

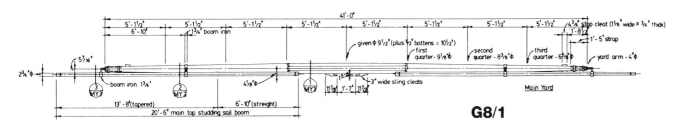

G8/1

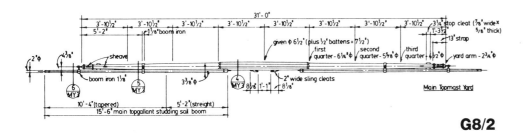

G8/2

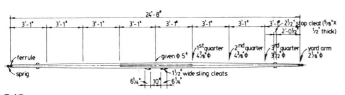

G8/3

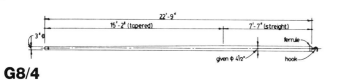

G8/4

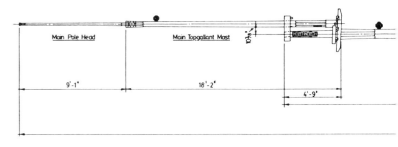

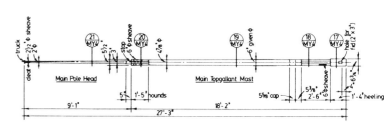

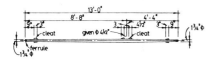

G8/5

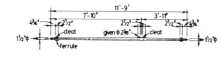

G8/6

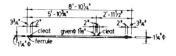

G8/7

G7/1 Mainmast assembly (1/96 scale)

G7/2 Main lower mast side and front elevation (1/96 scale)

G7/3 Main topmast (1/96 scale)

G7/4 Main topgallant and pole mast (1/96 scale)

G8 MAIN YARDS

G8/1 Main yard (1/96 scale)

G8/2 Main topyard (1/96 scale)

G8/3 Main topgallant yard (1/96 scale)

G8/4 Main lower studding sail boom (1/96 scale)

G8/5 Main studding sail yard (1/96 scale)

G8/6 Main top studding sail yard (1/96 scale)

G8/7 Main topgallant studding sail yard (1/96 scale)

G8/8 Main yard details (1/16 scale)
1. Main yard
2. Main yard quarter iron
3. Main yard studding sail boom iron

G8/9 Main topyard details (1/16 scale)
4. Main topyard
5. Main topyard quarter iron
6. Main topyard studding sail boom iron

G7/2

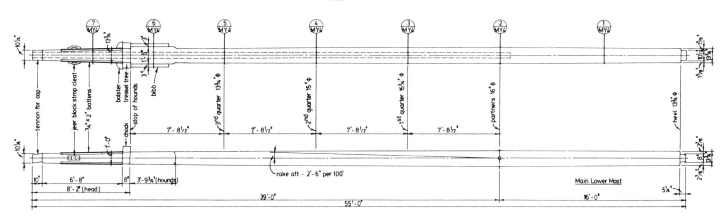

G7/1

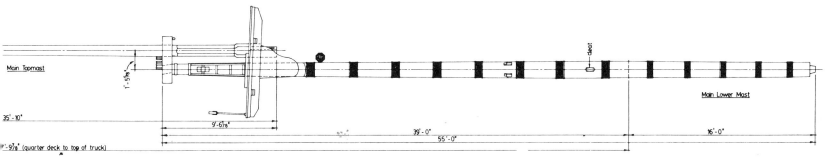

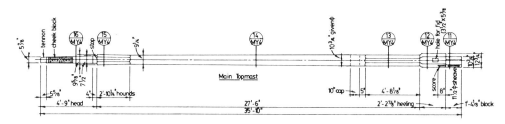

G8/8

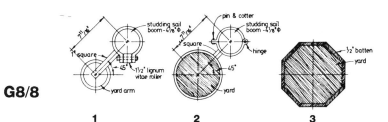

1   2   3

G8/9

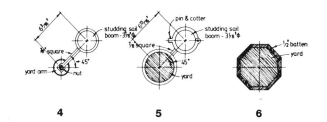

4   5   6

G Masts and spars

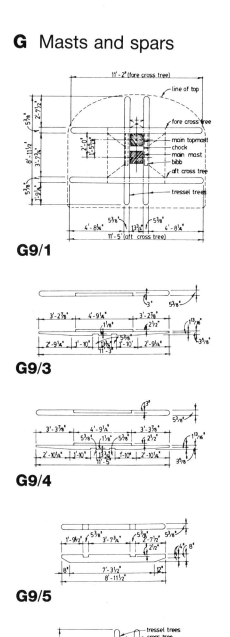

G9/1

G9/2

G9/3

G9/8

G9/4

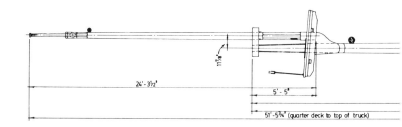

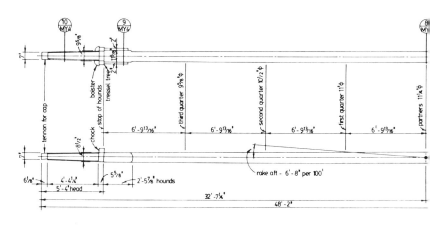

G9/5

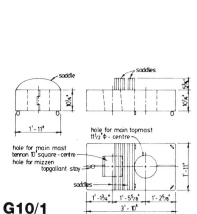

G10/1

G10/3

Main Topmast Cap

G9/6

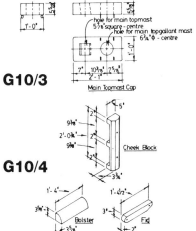

G10/4

Cheek Block

Bolster   *Fid*

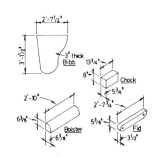
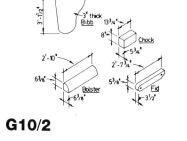

Bibb

Chock

Bolster   *Fid*

G10/2

G9/7

G9/5   Plan and elevation of main lower tressel trees (1/96 scale)

G9/6   Plan of main topmast top (1/48 scale)

G9/7   Plan and elevation of main top tressel trees (1/48 scale)

G9/8   Plan and elevation of main top cross trees (1/48 scale)

G10   MAINMAST DETAILS

G10/1   Main lower mast cap – plan, side elevation and front elevation (1/48 scale)

G10/2   Main lower mast – fid, bolster, chock and bibb (1/96 scale)

G10/3   Main topmast cap – plan, side elevation and front elevation (1/48 scale)

G10/4   Main topmast – fid, bolster and cheek block (1/48 scale)

G11   MIZZEN MAST

G11/1   Mizzen mast assembly (1/96 scale)

G11/2   Mizzen lower mast – front and side elevation

G11/3   Mizzen topmast (1/96 scale)

G9/1   Plan of main top trees (1/96 scale

G9/2   Plan of main top (1/96 scale)

G9/3   Plan and elevation of main lower cross trees (forward) (1/96 scale)

G9/4   Plan and elevation of main lower cross trees (aft) (1/96 scale)

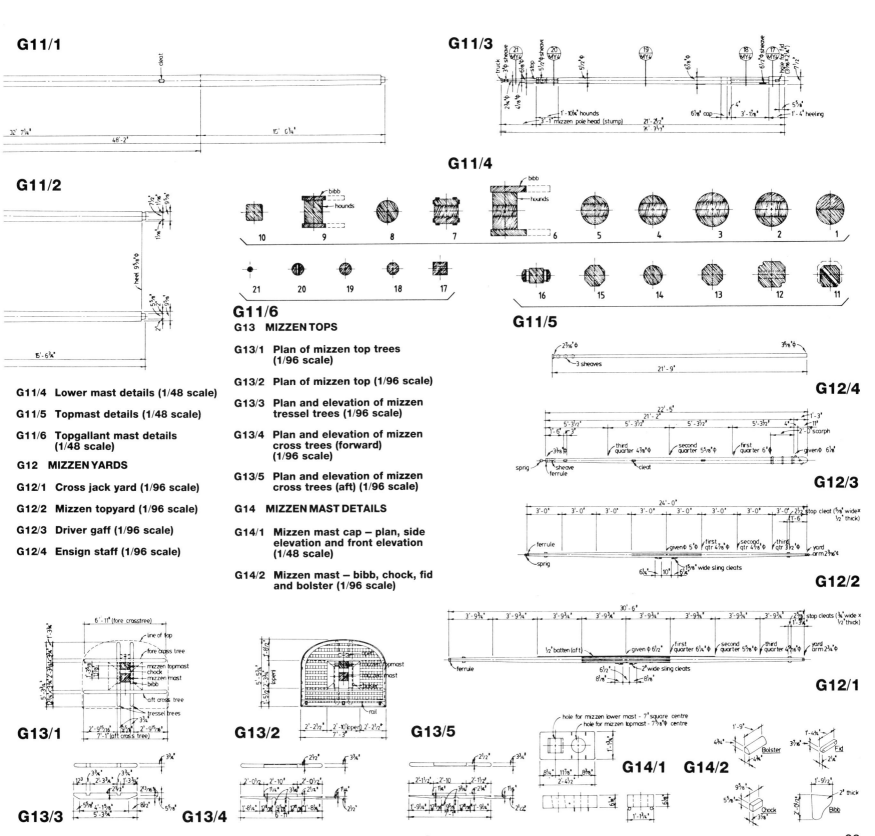

G11/1

32' 7¼"   48'-2"   15' 6¾"

cleat

G11/3

21 MYL   20 MYL   19 MYL   18 MYL   17 hole for fid
truck   3" φ sheave   stop   5½" φ sheave   5½" φ   6⅞"   6⅞"   6½" φ sheave   (3⅞" × 2½")

2¾" φ   4⅛" φ   1'-10¾" hounds   5½" φ   6⅞" cap   4"   5⅞" φ   1'-4" heeling
3'-1" mizzen pole head (stump)   21'-2½"   3'-1⅞"
24'-3½"

G11/4

bibb   bibb
hounds   hounds

10   9   8   7   6   5   4   3   2   1

21   20   19   18   17   16   15   14   13   12   11

G11/2

7½"   9⅜"
1⅛"
1¼"

heel 9⅝" φ

5⅝"
9⅝"
2"

5'-6¾"

G11/6

G13   MIZZEN TOPS

G13/1   Plan of mizzen top trees (1/96 scale)

G13/2   Plan of mizzen top (1/96 scale)

G13/3   Plan and elevation of mizzen tressel trees (1/96 scale)

G13/4   Plan and elevation of mizzen cross trees (forward) (1/96 scale)

G13/5   Plan and elevation of mizzen cross trees (aft) (1/96 scale)

G14   MIZZEN MAST DETAILS

G14/1   Mizzen mast cap – plan, side elevation and front elevation (1/48 scale)

G14/2   Mizzen mast – bibb, chock, fid and bolster (1/96 scale)

G11/4   Lower mast details (1/48 scale)

G11/5   Topmast details (1/48 scale)

G11/6   Topgallant mast details (1/48 scale)

G12   MIZZEN YARDS

G12/1   Cross jack yard (1/96 scale)

G12/2   Mizzen topyard (1/96 scale)

G12/3   Driver gaff (1/96 scale)

G12/4   Ensign staff (1/96 scale)

G11/5

2⁵⁄₁₆" φ   3⅝" φ
3 sheaves   21'-9"

G12/4

22'-5"
5'-3½"   5'-3½"   5'-3½"   5'-3½"   1'-3"
1'-6"   3"   11"   2'-0" scarph
third quarter 4⅞" φ   second quarter 5⅝" φ   first quarter 6"   given φ 6⅞"
3⅞" φ
sprig   sheave   cleat   ferrule

G12/3

24'-0"
3'-0"   3'-0"   3'-0"   3'-0"   3'-0"   3'-0"   3'-0"   3'-0"   2½" stop cleat (⅝" wide × ½" thick)
1'-6
ferrule   given φ 5" φ   first qtr 4⅞" φ   second qtr 4⅞" φ   third qtr 3½" φ   yard arm 2⅝" φ
sprig   6¼"   10"   6¼"   1⅝" wide sling cleats

G12/2

30'-6"
3'-9¾"   3'-9¾"   3'-9¾"   3'-9¾"   3'-9¾"   3'-9¾"   3'-9¾"   2⅝" stop cleats (⅜" wide × ½" thick)
1'-3¼
½" batten (aft)   given φ 6½"   first quarter 6¼" φ   second quarter 5⅝" φ   third quarter 4⅞" φ   yard arm 2¾" φ
ferrule   6½"   2" wide sling cleats
8⅞"   8⅞"

G12/1

G13/1

6'-11" (fore crosstree)
line of top
fore cross tree
mizzen topmast
chock
mizzen mast
bibb
aft cross tree
tressel trees
3¾"
2'-9¹⁵⁄₁₆"   5¼"   2'-9¹⁵⁄₁₆"
7'-1" (aft cross tree)

G13/2

(open)
1'-8½"
(open)   topmast   mizzen mast
5'-5¾" (open)
5½" (open)
rail
2'-2½"   2'-10" (open)   2'-2½"
7'-3"

G13/5

2½"   3¾"
2'-1½"   2'-10   2'-1½"
11¼"   3¾"   2½"
1'-9¾"   9⅝"   1'-8¼"   2½"

G14/1

hole for mizzen lower mast – 7" square centre
hole for mizzen topmast – 7⅝" φ centre
1'-1¼"
8¼"   11½"   8¼"
2'-4½"
1'-1¾"

G14/2

1'-9"
4¾"   3⁷⁄₁₆"   Bolster   1'-4½"   Fid   2¼"
4¾"   2¼"

9⅝"   1'-9½"
5⅝"   Chock   2" thick   Bibb
3⅝"   2'-0½"

G13/3
12¾   3¾"   3¾"   2⅜"   2³⁄₁₆"
2'-3¾"   3¾"
5⅝"   4'-1⅝"   8½"   5⅝"
5'-3¾"

G13/4
2½"   3¾"
2'-0½"   2'-10"   2'-0½"   1¼"   2½"
11¼"   3¾"   2½"
1'-8¼"   9⅝"   1'-8¼"   2½"

G Masts and spars

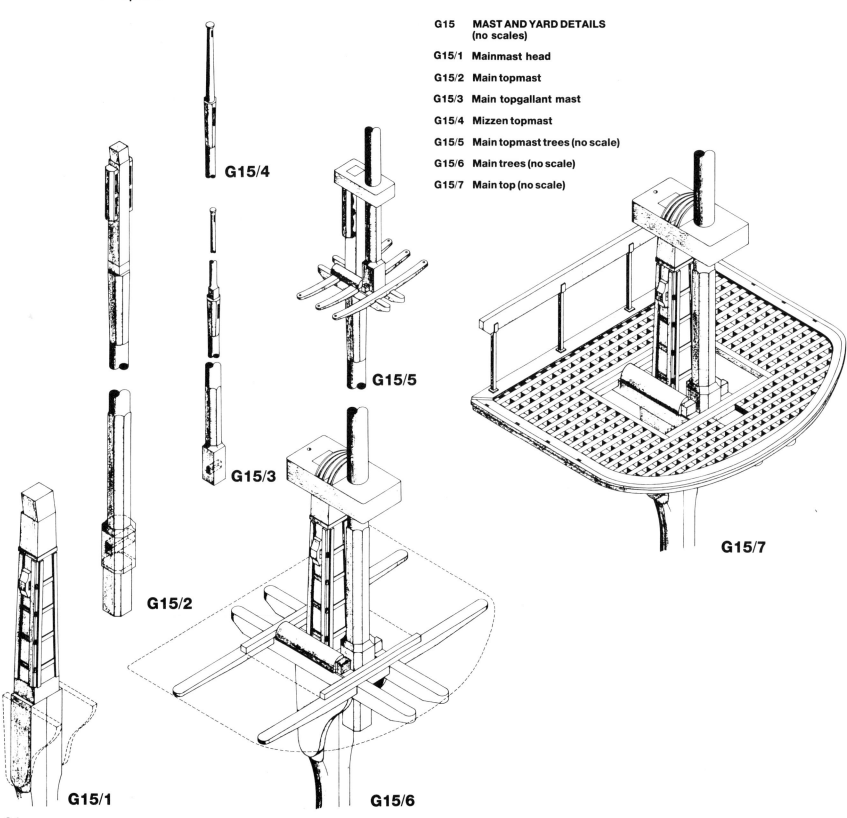

G15   **MAST AND YARD DETAILS**
(no scales)

G15/1   **Mainmast head**

G15/2   **Main topmast**

G15/3   **Main topgallant mast**

G15/4   **Mizzen topmast**

G15/5   **Main topmast trees (no scale)**

G15/6   **Main trees (no scale)**

G15/7   **Main top (no scale)**

G15/4

G15/3

G15/5

G15/7

G15/2

G15/1

G15/6

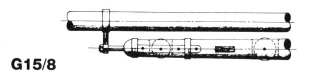

G15/8

G15/9

G15/8 Main yardarm

G15/9 Main topyard yardarm

G15/10 Main yard sling cleats

G15/11 Main yard

G15/12 Main yard boom iron

G15/13 Main yard yardarm

G15/14 Main topyard sling cleats

G15/15 Main topyard

G15/16 Main topyard boom iron

G15/17 Main topyard yardarm

G15/18 Main topgallant yard sling cleats

G15/19 Main topgallant yard yardarm

G15/20 Crossjack yard arm

G15/21 Detail of driver boom jaws

G15/22 Detail of driver boom and mizzen mast

G15/23 Detail of driver boom end

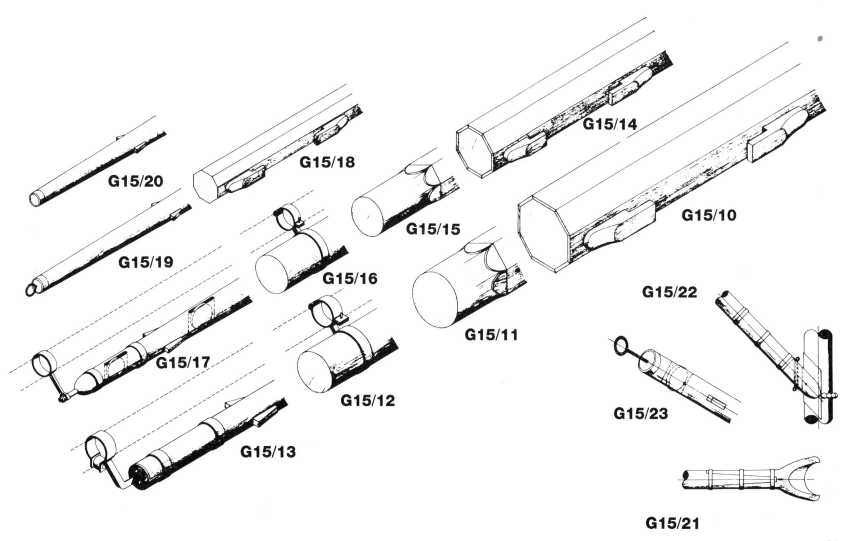

G15/20

G15/19

G15/17

G15/13

G15/18

G15/16

G15/12

G15/15

G15/11

G15/14

G15/10

G15/22

G15/23

G15/21

H Rigging

H1   **STANDING RIGGING**

H1/1   **Elevation of standing rigging**
         (1/192 scale)

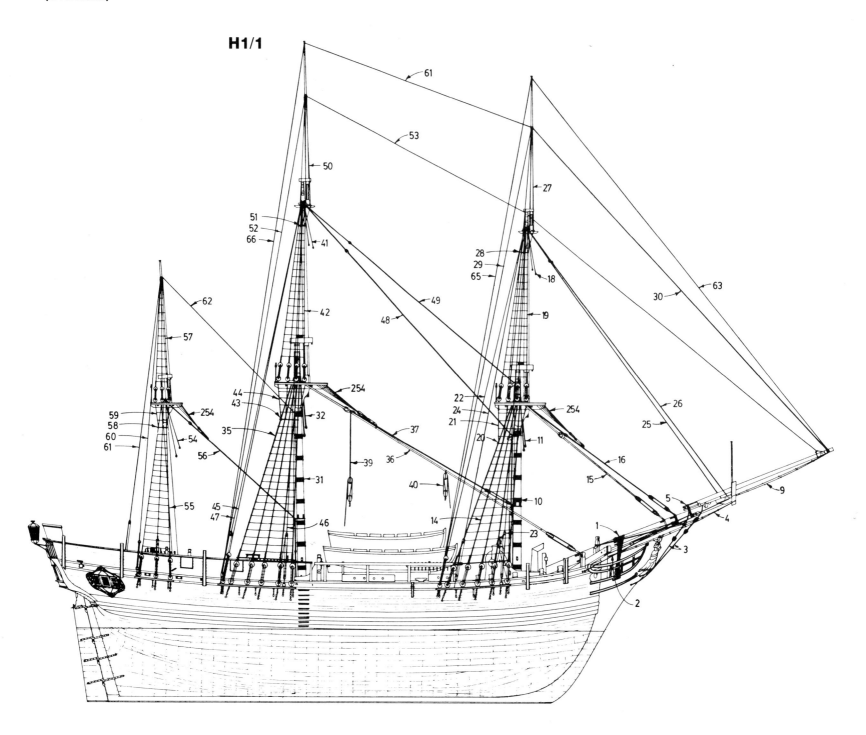

H1/1

H1/2

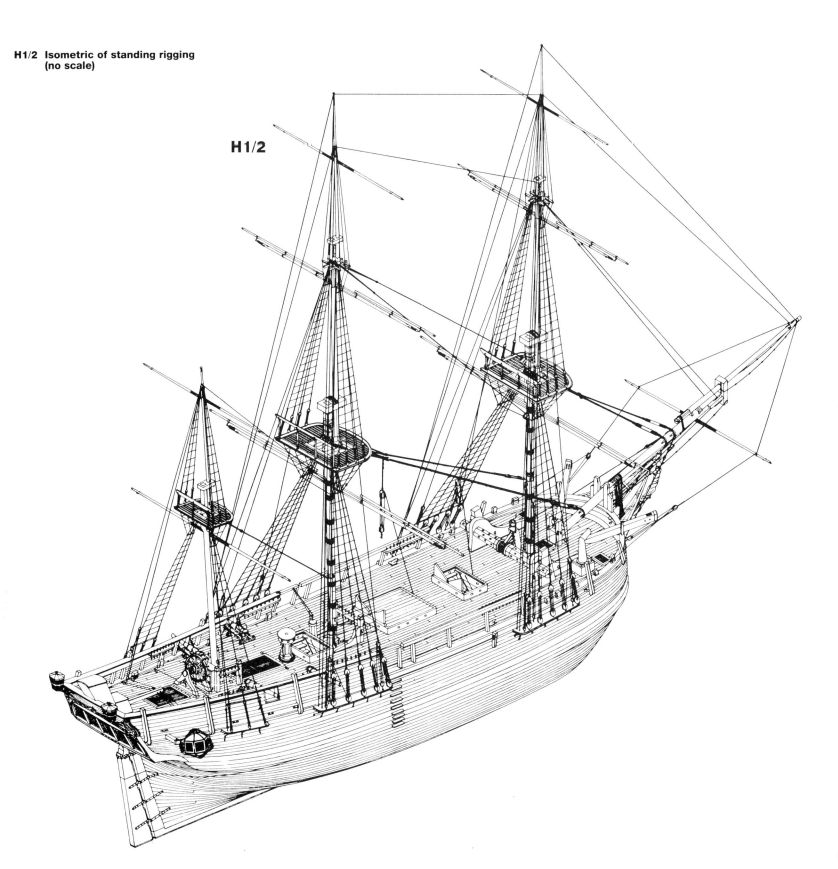

H1/3

H1/4

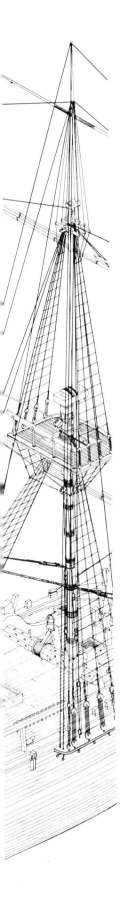

H1/5

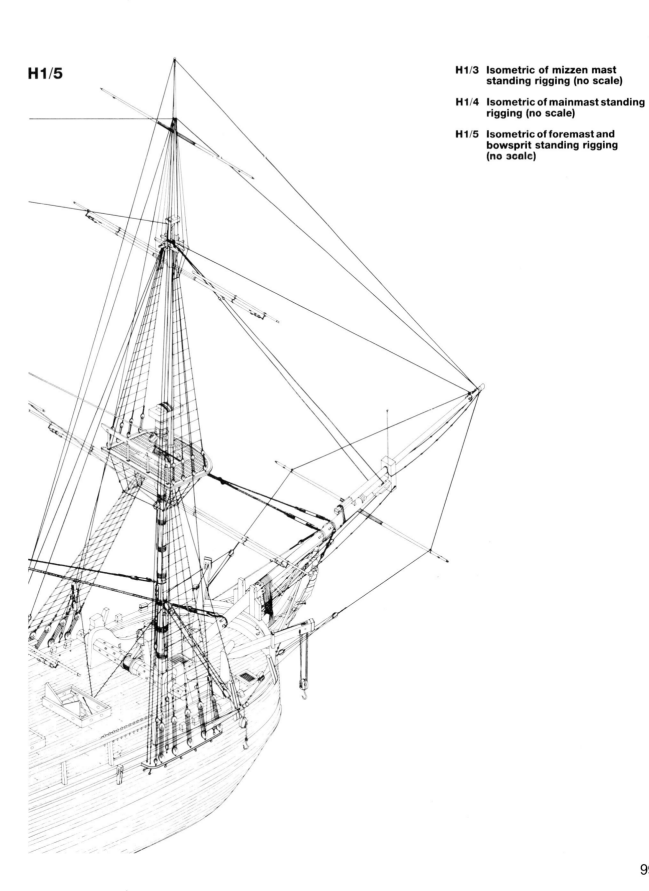

H1/3 Isometric of mizzen mast
      standing rigging (no scale)

H1/4 Isometric of mainmast standing
      rigging (no scale)

H1/5 Isometric of foremast and
      bowsprit standing rigging
      (no scale)

H Rigging

H2/1 Elevation of running rigging
      (1/192 scale)

H2/1

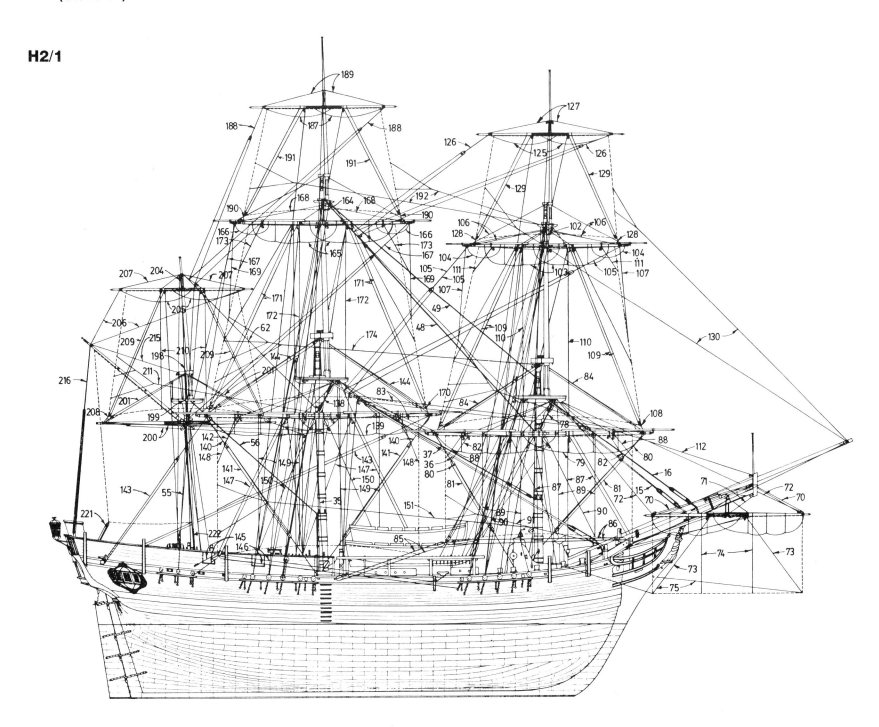

H2/2

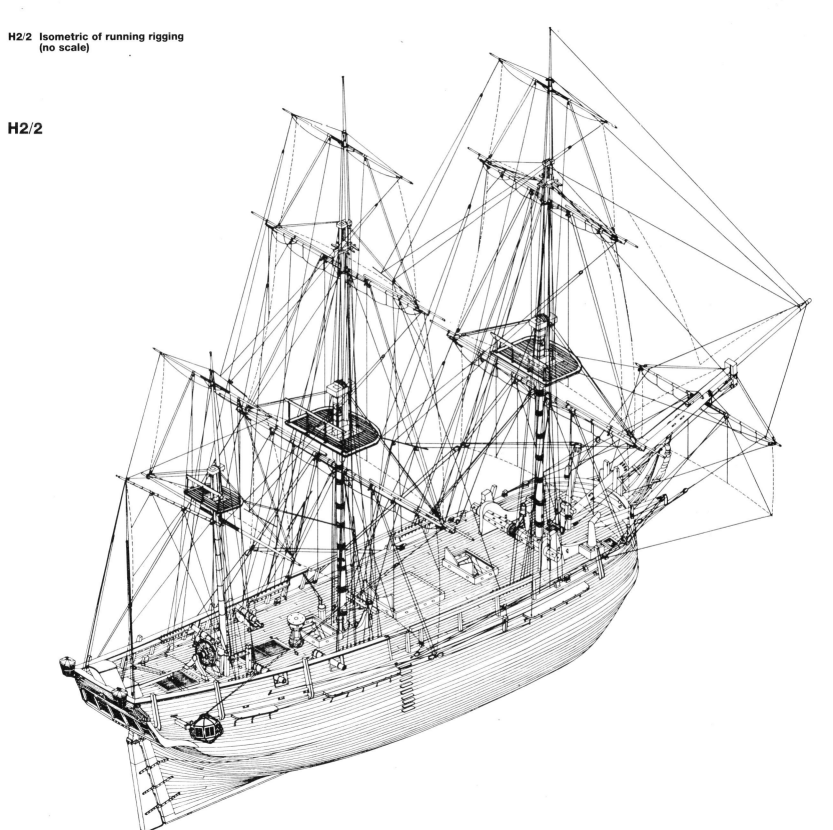

H2/5

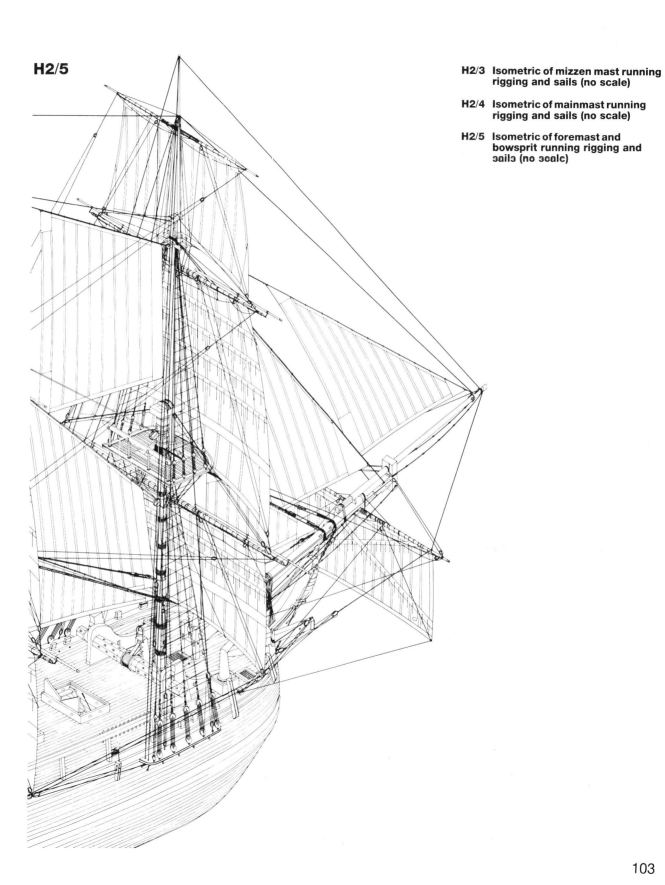

H2/3 Isometric of mizzen mast running
rigging and sails (no scale)

H2/4 Isometric of mainmast running
rigging and sails (no scale)

H2/5 Isometric of foremast and
bowsprit running rigging and
sails (no scale)

H3/1   Foremast rigging (1/192 scale)

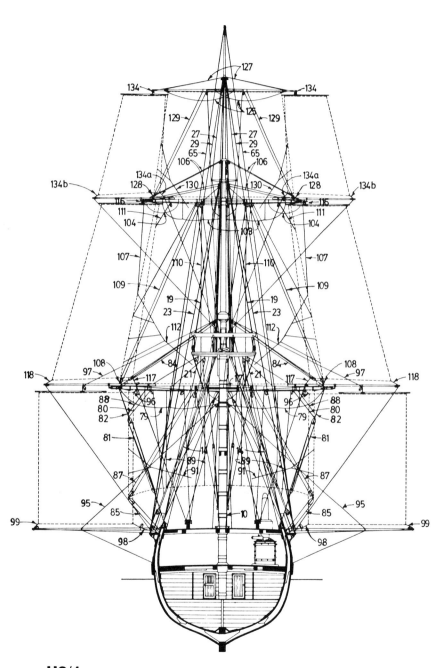

H3/1

H4/1 Mainmast rigging (1/192 scale)

H5/1 Mizzen mast rigging (1/192 scale)

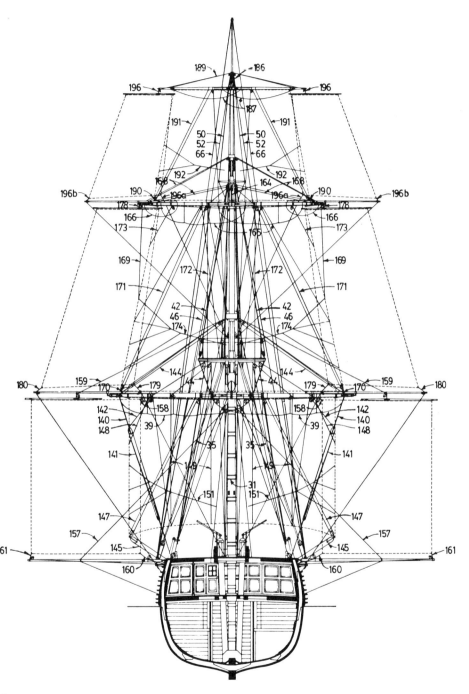

H4/1

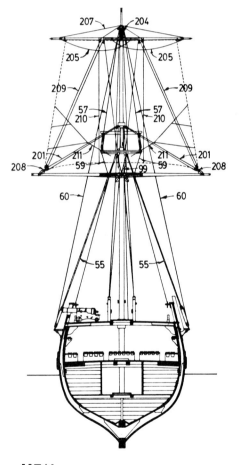

H5/1

H Rigging

H6/1 Belaying plan (1/128 scale)

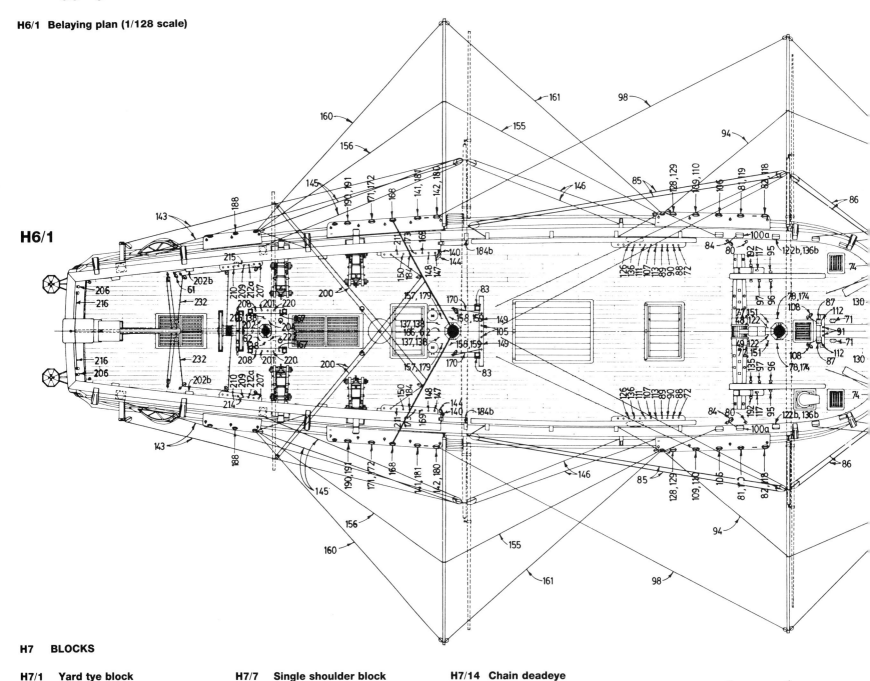

H6/1

H7 BLOCKS

H7/1	**Yard tye block**	**H7/7**	**Single shoulder block**	**H7/14**	**Chain deadeye**
H7/2	**Sheet quarter block**	**H7/8**	**Clew garnet**	**H7/15**	**Shroud deadeye**
H7/3	**Yard tackle blocks**	**H7/9**	**Long tackle block**	**H7/16**	**Closed heart**
H7/4	**Stay block**	**H7/10**	**Sister blocks**	**H7/17**	**Bull's eye**
H7/5	**Leechline and spritsail brace block**	**H7/11**	**Mizzen euphroe**	**H7/18**	**Shroud tuck**
		H7/12	**Fore euphroe**	**H7/19**	**Shroud cleat**
H7/6	**Common single and double blocks**	**H7/13**	**Main euphroe**	**H7/20**	**Parral**

H7/14

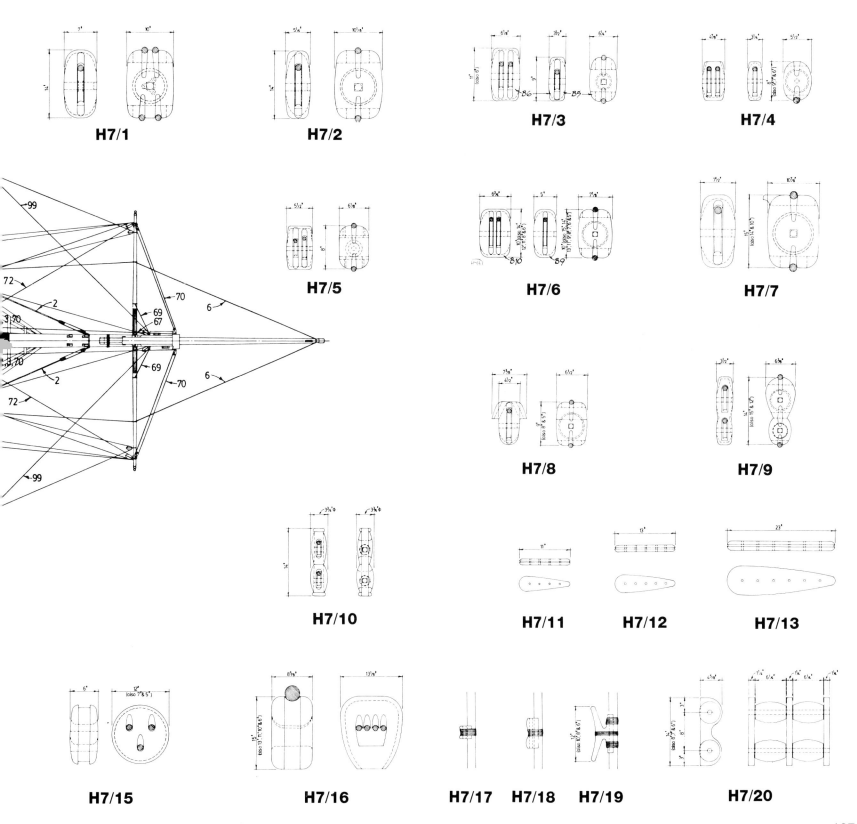

H7/1

H7/2

H7/3

H7/4

H7/5

H7/6

H7/7

H7/8

H7/9

H7/10

H7/11

H7/12

H7/13

H7/15

H7/16

H7/17

H7/18

H7/19

H7/20

H8/1 Rigging schedule

Standing Rigging

Item & No	Name	Quantity	Circumference	Length (Fathoms)	Notes	Blocks/Hearts Type	Blocks/Hearts Size	Notes	Belays To
	Bowsprit								
1	Gammoning	1 Set	4½"	34				11 Turns	
2	Shrouds	1 pr	4½"	8½	Cable-laid	H	6"	2 Hearts 2 Eyebolts	
Shrouds	Collar	1	3½"	2⅞	wormed, parcelled & Served	H	6"	2 Hearts	
	Seizings	2	¾"	7					
	Lashings	2	1"	3⅞					
	Lanyards	2	2"	5¾					Forecastle
3	Bobstays	2	5"	11¾	wormed, parcelled & Served for ¼	H	6"	2 Hearts	
Bobstays	Collars	2	5"	3	wormed, parcelled & Served	H	6"	2 Hearts	
	Seizings	2	¾"	11¾					
	Lashings	2	1"	4					
	Lanyards	2	2½"	6					Forcastle
4	Horses	2	3"	10	Knots cast at 3' %			6 Thimbles, 4 Eyebolts	
	Lanyards	2	1"	3¾					
	Jib Boom								
5	Heel Lashing	1	2½"	7				4 Turns	
6	Guy Pendants	2	2½"	16⅞		B10	10"	2 Blocks	
Guy Pendants	Falls	2	1½"	18⅞		B9	9"	2 Blocks	Forecastle
	Strapping	2	2½"		From Guy Pend.				
	Lashers	2	¾"	8½					
7	Outhauler *	1	2"	6¾					
	Tackle Fall	1	2"	6⅛		B9	6"	2 Blocks	Forecastle
	Strapping	1	1½"	1					
8	Strap *	1	3"	1	wormed, parcelled & served			3 Thimbles	
9	Horses	2	3"	10¾	Knots cast at 3' %				
	Seizings	2		5⅜					
	Fore Mast								
10	Wooldings	12	2½"	127½	13 Turns				
11	Pendents of Tackles	1 pr.	7"	5	cabled - wormed, parcelled & served	B9	15"	2 Blocks, 4 Thimbles	
	Strapping		4½"	1⅔					
	Seizing		¾"	5					
12	Runners of Tackles *	2	4"	20					
	Strapping		3½"	2					
13	Falls of Tackles *	2	2½"	51		B9, 13"	B9, 9"	2 of each Block	
	Strapping	2	3½"	2½					
	Seizing	2	¾"	10					
14	Shrouds	4 pr.	7"	62¼	wormed, parcelled & Served	D1	12"	10 Deadeyes	Sheer Pole
	Swifters	1 pr.	7"			D2	12"	10 Deadeyes	
Shrouds	Eye Seizing	4	1"	15½					
	Throat Seizing	10	1"	31					
	End Seizing	10	¾"	31					
	Lanyard	10	3½"	39					
	Ratlines		1½"	39					
15	Fore Stay	1	9½"	7¼	cabled, 4 strand, wormed, parcelled & served	H	13"	Eye & Mouse	
Fore Stay	Seizings	3	1"	14¼					
	Lanyard	1	3½"	7¼					
	Collar (Double)	1	5"	3⅝	cabled, 4 strand, wormed, parcelled & served	H	13"		
	Seizings	2	1"	5½					
	Lashings		1½"	2¾					
16	Preventer Stay	1	6"	7¼	cabled, 4 strand, wormed, parcelled & served	H	10"	Eye & Mouse	
Preventer Stay	Lanyard	1	2½"	4⅞					
	Collar (Double)	1	4"	3⅝	cabled, 4 Strand, wormed, parcelled & served	H	10"		
	Lashing		1"	3⅝					
	Seizings		1"	9					
17	Catharpin Legs	2	3½"	2½	wormed, parcelled & served				
	Seizing		¾"	10					
	Fore Topmast								
18	Burton Pendents	1 pr.	3"	3⅞	wormed, parcelled & served	B9	6"	2 Blocks, 2 Thimbles	
	Falls	2	1½"	34		B10	6"	2 Blocks	
	Strapping		1½"	2⅞					
19	Shrouds	4 pr.	4½"	42	wormed, parcelled & served	D1	7"	8 Deadeyes	
Shrouds	Eye Seizing	8	¾"	10½		D2	7"	8 Deadeyes	
	Throat Seizing	8	¾"	18⅜					
	End Seizing	8	¾"	15¾					
	Lanyards	8	2½"	28					
	Ratlines		1"	15					
20	Futtock Staves	1 pr	3"		Served			Oak Batten	
21	Futtock Shrouds	4 pr	4½"	15⅜	Served				
Futtock Shrouds	Upper Seizing	8	¾"	19⅝					
	Lower Seizing	8	¾"	17¼					
	Ratlines		1"	4					
22	Standing Backstay	1 pr	4½"	22⅞	Tarred Line	D1	7"	2 Deadeyes	
Standing Backstays	Eye Seizing	2	½"	2⅞	Tarred Line	D2	7"	2 Deadeyes	
	Throat Seizing	4	½"	5	Tarred Line				
	End Seizing	4	½"	4⅜	Tarred Line				
	Lanyards	2	2½"	4½					
23	Breast Backstay	1 pr.	3"	21¼	Wormed & Served	B7	7"	2 Single Blocks	
Breast Backstay	Runners	2	3"	4½		B7	7"	2 Double Blocks	
	Falls	2	2"	11½					
	Strapping		2½"	2					

* Not Shown on Drawings

Standing Rigging

Item & No	Name	Quantity	Circumference	Length (Fathoms)	Notes	Blocks/Hearts Type	Blocks/Hearts Size	Notes	Belays To
24	Shifting Backstay	1 pr.	4½"	21½		B7	8"	2 Double Blocks	
	Tackles	2	2"	25⅜		B7	8"	2 Single Blocks	
	Strapping	2	3"	5⅜				2 Thimbles	
25	Stay	1	5"	13¾	cable laid, 4 strand - wormed, parcelled & Served	B13	15"	Eye & Mouse	
Stay	Collar	1	4"	2¼					
	Tackle		2½"	13¾		B9	8"		
	Strapping		3"	2					
	Seizing		¾"	4					
26	Preventer Stay	1	4"	13¾	cable laid, 4 strand - wormed, parcelled & Served	B13	14"	Eye & Mouse	
Preventer Stay	Collar	1	3"	1¾					
	Tackle		2"	12		B9	8"		
	Strapping		3"	2					
	Seizing		¾"	6					
	Collar Lashing		1"	3½					
	Fore Topgallant Mast								
27	Shrouds	3 pr	2½"	45⅓				12 Thimbles	Fore Top
	Lanyards	6	1"	7⅝					
28	Futtock Staves	1 pr	1½"		Served			Oak Batten	
29	Standing Backstay	1 pr	2½"	27⅛				4 Thimbles	Fore Channel
	Lanyards	2	1"	6¾					
30	Stay	1	3"	19¾	cabled - 4 Strand			1 Thimble	Gammoning with Lanyard
	Strapping		2½"	1					
	Main Mast								
31	Wooldings	13	2½"	137½	13 Turns				
32	Pendents of Tackles	1 pr	7"	4½	cabled - wormed, parcelled & Served	B9	15"	2 Blocks, 4 Thimbles	
	Strapping	2	4½"	1½					
	Seizing	2	¾"	4½					
33	Runners of Tackles *	2	4"	18					
	Seizing		3½"	3					
34	Falls of Tackles *	2	2½"	55		B9, 13"	B9, 9"	2 of each Block	
	Strapping	2	3½"	2¾					
	Seizing	2	¾"	11					
35	Shrouds	4 pr.	7"	65	wormed, parcelled & Served	D1	12"	10 Deadeyes	Sheer Pole
	Swifters	1 pr	7"			D2	12"	10 Deadeyes	
Shrouds	Eye Seizing	4	1"	16¼					
	Throat Seizing	10	1"	32½					
	End Seizing	10	¾"	32½					
	Lanyards	10	3½"	40⅜					
	Ratlines		1½"	46					
36	Main Stay	1	10"	11	cabled, 4 strand, wormed, parcelled & Served	H	15"	Eye & Mouse	
Main Stay	Seizings	3	1½"	11					
	Lanyards	1	3½"	8¼					
	Collar	1	8"	5½	cabled, 4 strand, wormed, parcelled & Served	H	15"		
	Seizing	2	1"	9⅝					
	Lashings		2	11					
37	Preventer Stay	1	7"	9	cabled, 4 strand, wormed, parcelled & served	H	11"	Eye & Mouse	
Preventer Stay	Lanyard	1	3"	4½					
	Collar	1	4½"	3	cabled, 4 strand, wormed, parcelled & served	H	11"		
	Lashing		2"	3					
	Seizing		1"	9					
38	Catharpin Legs *	2	3½"	2½	wormed, parcelled & Served				
	Seizing		¾"	10					
39	Stay Tackle Pendant	1	5"	2¾		B10	12"	2 Thimbles	
Main Stay Pendant	Falls		3"	24¾		B9	13"		
	Strapping		3½"	2					
	Seizing		¾"	8¼					
	Lashing		1½"	6¼					
40	Fore Hatch Tackle	1	3"	2¾		B10	12"	2 Thimbles	
Fore Hatch Tackle	Fall		3"	24¾		B9	13"		
	Strapping		3½"	2					
	Seizing		¾"	8¼					
	Main Topmast								
41	Burton Pendants	1 pr	3"	4	wormed, parcelled & served	B9	6"	2 Blocks, 2 Thimbles	
	Falls	2	1½"	36		B10	6"	2 Blocks	
	Strapping		2"	2⅔					
42	Shrouds	4 pr	4½"	42	wormed, parcelled & served	D1	7"	8 Deadeyes	
Shrouds	Eye Seizing		¾"	10½		D2	7"	8 Deadeyes	
	Throat Seizing		¾"	18⅜					
	End Seizing		¾"	15¾					
	Lanyards		2½"	25¾					
	Ratlines		1"	16					
43	Futtock Staves	1 pr.	3"		Served			Oak Batten	
44	Futtock Shrouds	4 pr.	4½"	15¾	Served				
Futtock Shrouds	Upper Seizing	8	¾"	21					
	Lower Seizing	8	¾"	18⅞					
	Ratlines		1	4					
45	Standing Backstay	1 pr.	4½"	24	Tarred Line	D1	7"	2 Deadeyes	
Standing Backstay	Eye Seizing	2	½"	3	Tarred Line	D2	7"	2 Deadeyes	
	Throat Seizing	4	½"	5¼	Tarred Line				
	End Seizing	4	½"	4½	Tarred Line				
	Lanyards	2	2½"	4⅞					

Standing Rigging

Item & No	Name	Quantity	Circumference	Length (Fathoms)	Notes	Blocks/Hearts Type	Blocks/Hearts Size	Notes	Belays To
46	Breast Backstay	1pr	3"	22 3/8	wormed & served	B7	9"	2 Single Blocks	
	Runners	2	2"	4 5/8		B7	7"	2 Double Blocks	
Breast Backstay	Falls	2	2"	12					
	Strapping		2½"	2					
47	Shifting Backstay	1pr	4½"	22½		B7	8"	2 Double Blocks	
	Tackles	2	2"	20		B7	8"	2 Single Blocks	
	Strapping	2	2"	3				2 Thimbles	
48	Stay	1	5½"	14½	cable laid, 4 strand wormed, parcelled & served	B13	15"	Eye & Mouse	
	Collar	1	4"	2½		B9	14"	Thimble	
	Tackle	1	2½"	14½		B9	7"		Foot of Fore Mast
	Strapping		3"	2½					
Stay	Seizing		¾"	4 7/8"					
	Lashing		1"	6					
49	Preventer Stay	1	4"	14½	cable laid, 4 strand wormed, parcelled & served	B13	12"	Eye & Mouse	Foot of Foremast
	Collar	1	3"	2½		B9	11"		
	Tackle	1	1½"	14½		B9	6"		
	Strapping		3"	1 7/8					
Preventer Stay	Seizing		¾"	5½					
	Lashing the Collar		1"	3 5/8					
	Main Topgallant Mast								
50	Shrouds	3pr	2½"	48				12 Thimbles	Main Top
	Lanyard	6	1"	8					
51	Futtock Staves	1pr.	1½"		Served			Oak Batten	
52	Standing Backstay	1pr	2½"	28½				4 Thimbles	Main Channel
	Lanyards	2	1"	7 1/8					
53	Stay	1	3"	14½	cabled - 4 Strand			1 Thimble	Fore Mast
	Strapping		2½"	1					Tressel Trees
	Mizzen Mast								
54	Pendents of Tackles	1pr.	3½"	6	wormed, parcelled & served			2 Thimbles	
	Falls	2	2"	36		B9, 8"	B12, 8"	2 of each Block	
	Strapping		2"	3					
55	Shrouds	2pr.	4½"	30	wormed, parcelled & served	D1	7"	6 Deadeyes	Sheer Pole
	Swifters	1pr	4½"			D2	7"	6 Deadeyes	
	Eye Seizings	2	¾"	7½					
	Throat Seizings	6	¾"	15					
Shrouds	End Seizings	6	¾"	11¼					
	Lanyards	6	2½"	15					
	Ratlines		1"	19½					
56	Stay	1	5½"	8	cabled, 4 strand, wormed, parcelled & served			eye & mouse 2 Thimbles	Foot of Main Mast
	Seizings	3	¾"	4					
	Lanyard	1	2½"	5					
	Collar	1	4"	2½					
Stay	Seizings	2	¾"	3					
	Lashing		¾"	3					
	Mizzen Topmast								
57	Shrouds	3pr.	2½"	21¼	wormed, parcelled & served	D1	5"	6 Deadeyes	
Shrouds	Seizings		¾"	31 7/8		D2	5"	6 Deadeyes	
	Lanyards	6	1½"	14 1/8					
	Ratlines		¾"	7⅓					
58	Futtock Staves	1pr.	1½"		Served			Oak Batten	
59	Futtock Shrouds	3pr	2½"	6 3/8	Served				
	Seizings		¾"	42½					
	Ratlines		¾"	1½					
60	Standing Backstay	1pr.	2½"	16 1/8	Tarred Line	D1	5"	4 Deadeyes	
	Seizing	2	¾"	8					
	Lanyards	2	1½"	8					
61	Shifting Backstay	2	2½"	8¼		B7	6"	2 Blocks 2 Thimbles	Quarter Deck
	Tackle	2	1½"	10					
	Strapping		2"	3					
62	Stay	1	3"	7¼					Foot of Main Mast
Stay	Lanyard	1	1½"	3 5/8				2 Thimbles	
	Collar	1	2"	1 7/8"				1 Thimble	
	Flagstaff Stays								
63	Fore Flagstaff Stay	1	1½"	18					Fore Stay Collar
	Collar	1	1"	1	1 Thimble				
64	Main Flagstaff Stay	1	1½"	17½					Fore Top
	Collar	1	1"	1	1 Thimble				
	Flagstaff Backstays								
65	Fore Flagstaff Backstay	1pr	1½"	10¼	2 Thimbles				Fore Channel
	Lanyard	2	¾"	18	2 Thimbles & 2 Eyebolts				
	Strapping		¾"	1					
66	Main Flagstaff Backstay	1pr	1½"	10 7/8					
	Lanyard	2	¾"	21½	2 Thimbles & 2 Eyebolts				Main Channel
	Strapping		¾"	1½					

Running Rigging

Item & No	Name	Quantity	Circumference	Length (Fathoms)	Notes	Blocks/Hearts Type	Blocks/Hearts Size	Notes	Belays To
	Spritsail Yard & Sail								
67	Slings	1pr	3½"	2 7/8					
	Seizing & Racking		¾"	5¾					
68	Horses	2	2½"	5 5/8				4 Thimbles	
	Stirrups	6	2	2 7/8					
69	Lifts, Standing	2	2½"	4				4 Thimbles	
Lifts	Straps	2	2"	2					
	Lanyards	2	¾"	3					
70	Lifts	2	2"	24½		B9	7"	2 Blocks	Forecastle
	Beckets		2"	2					
Lifts	Strapping		2"	2		B9	7"	2 Blocks	
	Seizing		¾"	4					
71	Halyard	1	2"	16 1/8		B9	7"	2 Blocks	Forecastle
Halyard	Strapping		2½"	2		C	10"	2 Cleats	
	Seizing & Lashing		¾"	3 7/8					
72	Braces	2	2½"	35		B8	9"	4 Blocks	Forerail
Braces	Pendants	2	3"	3		B9	9"	2 Blocks	
	Strapping	2	3"	5					
73	Cluelines	2	1½"	18 5/8					Forecastle
	Strapping	2	1½"	2⅓		B9	6"	2 Blocks	
74	Buntlines	2	1"	14	Single				Forecastle
	Strapping	2	1½	1					
75	Sheets	2	3"	17½	Cabled, single				Forecastle
76	Ear-rings *	2	1"	7					
	Fore Yard & Sail								
77	Truss Pendant	2	4½"	6⅓		B10	8"	4 Thimbles, 2 Blocks	
	Falls	2	2"	23¾		B10	8"	2 Blocks	Cleat on Mast
Truss Pendant	Strapping		2½"	3 1/8					
	Eye Seizing	2	¾"	9 3/8					
	Nave Line	1	1"	7 5/8		B9	6"		Foot of Fore Mast
78	Jeer Falls	2	2½"	51		B1	20"	3 Blocks	Foot of Fore Mast
	Strapping		5", 4", 2½"	6 7/8		B10	12"	4 Blocks	
	Seizing		1	12¾					
Jeers	Lashing, Masthead	2	3"	22 7/8					
	Lashing, Yard	2	2"	7 5/8					
	Tye	2	7"	10		B1	12"	2 Blocks	
79	Horses	2	3½"	6⅓				2 Thimbles	
	Stirrups	6	2½"	6⅓				6 Thimbles	
	Lanyard		1"	6⅓					
80	Yard Tackle Pendants	2	4½"	3 7/8		B6	11"	2 Blocks	Forecastle
	Falls	2	2½"	38		B5	9"	2 Blocks	
	Strapping		3"	3 7/8					
81	Inner Tricing Line	2	1½"	16¼		B9	6"	2 Blocks, C8" 2 Reqd	Fore Shrouds
82	Outer Tricing Line	2	1½"	16¼		B9	6"	4 Blocks	Fore Shrouds
	Strapping		1½"	2¾		C	8"	2 Cleats	
83	Braces	2	2½"	44⅓		B9	9"	2 Blocks	Fore Brace Bitts
	Pendants		3½"	4¾		B9	9"	2 Blocks	
Braces	Preventer		2½"	5¾					
	Strapping	2	2½"	2 7/8					
	Lashing		¾"	9½					
84	Lifts	2	3"	47½		B9	9"	4 Blocks	Forecastle
	Span for the Cap	1	4"	3 7/8		B13	14"	2 Blocks	
Lifts	Short Span		3"	1¼					
	Strapping		3"	2½					
85	Sheets	2	4"	38	cabled	B4	14"	2 Blocks, 2 Thimbles	Waist
	Strapping		4"			B9	14"	2 Blocks	Eyebolts
Sheets	Seizings		¾"	6⅓					
	Stoppers	2	3"	2 1/8					
86	Tacks	2	5"	33¼	Taper & Cabled	B11	14"	2 Blocks	Fore Castle
	Strapping		4"	4		B9	14"	2 Blocks	
	Seizing		¾"	6 5/8					
87	Clue Garnets	2	2½"	28½		B12	9"	2 Blocks	Fore Topsail sheet Bitts
	Straps		2½"	3½		B9	9"	2 Blocks	
	Strapping		2½"	1					
88	Leechline Legs	2	2"	21¾		B8	9"	4 Blocks - with 72	Fore Rail
	Falls	2	2"	21¾		B9	9"	4 Blocks	
	Strapping		2½"	5½					
89	Buntline Legs	4	2"	24¾		B10	8"	2 Blocks	Fore Rail
	Falls	4	2"	24¾		B9	8"	8 Blocks	
	Strapping		2½"	5½					
90	Slablines	2	1½"	14¼		B9	6"	2 Blocks	Fore Rail
	Strapping		1½"	2					
91	Bowlines	2	3"	25⅓		B9	11"	2 Blocks	Fore Topsail Sheet Bitts
	Bridles	2	3"	2½				2 Thimbles	
	Strapping		3"	1 7/8					
	Lashing		1"	3¾	Fore Stay Collar	B9	11"	2 Blocks	
92	Earrings *	2	1½"	12 5/8					
	Fore Lower Studding Sail								
93	Fore Guy	2	2"	23		B9	7"	2 Blocks	Fore Castle
	Strapping	2	2"	1					

Item & No	Name	Quantity	Circumference	Length (Fathoms)	Notes	Blocks/Hearts Type	Blocks/Hearts Size	Notes	Belays To
	Running Rigging								
94	After Guy	2	2"	24		B9	7"	2 Blocks	Fore Channel
	Strapping	2	2"	1					
95	Topping Lift	2	2½"	15½		B9	8"	2 Blocks	
	Span	1	3"	5		C	10"	2 Cleats	Carrick Bitts
96	Inner Halyard	2	2"	22 7/8		B9	9"	4 Blocks.C10",2	Carrick Bitts
97	Outer Halyard	2	2½"	38		B9	9"	4 Blocks.C,10",2	Carrick Bitts
98	Sheets	2	2"	6⅓		B9	9"	2 Blocks	Main Channel
99	Tacks	2	2½"	27		B9	9"	4 Blocks	Fore Castle
	Strapping		2½"	6⅓					
	Fore Stay Sail								
100	Staysail Halyard	1	2"	16½		B9	8"	2 Blocks	Forecastle
100a	Sheets	2	2½"	14½		B9	8"	2 Blocks	Forecastle
100b	Tack		1½"	2					Forecastle
100c	Down Hauler	1	1½"	14½		B9	6"	1 Block	Forecastle
	Strapping		1½"	2½					
	Fore Top Yard & Sail								
101	Parral Ropes *	2	2"	5 3/8				14" Parral	
102	Tie *	1	4"	25 5/8					Fore Channel, St'bd
	Strapping		4"	5 1/8	served				
	Seizing		¾"	7¾					
Tie	Lashers, Mast	2	1½"	6 7/8	served	B3	14"	1 Block	
	Lashers, Yard		1"	3½	served				
103	Horses	2	3"	5 3/8					
	Stirrups	4	2"	4¼				4 Thimbles	
104	Flemish Horse	2	3"						
105	Braces	2	2"	46⅓		B9	8"	4 Blocks	Fore Brace Bitts
	Pendants		3"	4⅔		B9	8"	2 Blocks	
	Strapping	2	2"	2⅓					
106	Lifts	2	2½"	31½		B14	14"	2 Blocks, with 107	Fore Shrouds
	Beckets	2	2½"	2		B9	8"	2 Blocks.C,12",2	
	Strapping		2½"	6		B9	8"	4 Blocks	
107	Reef Tackle Pend'ts	2	2½"	21		B9	7"	4 Blocks	Fore Rail
	Falls	2	1½"	28		B14	14"	2 Blocks, with 106	
	Strapping		2"	1½					
108	Sheets	2	4"	24½					
	Straps, Blocks	2	4½"	2½		B11	14"	2 Blocks	Fore Topsail Sheet Bitts
	Straps, Quarter Blocks	2	3½"	3¾		B4	14"	2 Blocks	
	Lashers, Quarter Blocks	2	1"	5		B9	14"	2 Blocks	
	Seizing	2	¾"	9 1/8					
Sheets	Span		3"	4					
	Stoppers	2	3"	2					
109	Clue Lines	2	2"	42		B12	8"	2 Blocks	Fore Shrouds
	Strapping		2½"	4¼		B9	8"	2 Blocks.C,10",2	
110	Bunt Lines	2	2"	32		B9	7"	2 Blocks.C,10",2	Fore Shrouds
	Strapping		2"	2		B9	7"	2 Blocks	
111	Leech Lines	2	1½"	13		B9	6"	2 Blocks	Fore Rail
	Strapping		1½"	1					
112	Bow Lines	2	2"	27		B9	8"	2 Blocks	Fore Topsail Sheet Bitts
	Bridles	4	2"	7				4 Thimbles	
	Strapping		2"	1					
Bow Lines	Lashing		¾"	7					
113	Halyards *	2	2½"	68½		B10	14"	2 Blocks	Fore Rail
	Strapping		3½"	4 7/8		B9	14"	2 Blocks	
	Seizing		¾"	9¾					
114	Slings *	1	3"	5 3/8					
115	Earrings *	2	1"	21					
	Fore Top Studding Sail								
116	Halyards	2	2"	46⅓		B9	8"	6 Blocks	Fore Top
117	Sheets	2	1½"	23⅓		B9	8"	2 Blocks.C,10",2	Carrick Bitts
118	Tacks	2	2"	32⅔		B9	8"	2 Blocks	Fore Channel
119	Downhaulers *	2	1"	28		B9	6"	2 Blocks	Fore Channel
120	Tails		2"	9⅓					
121	Straps		2"	3 1/8					
	Fore Top Stay Sail								
122	Staysail Stay	1	2½"	14¾		B9	9"	1 Block	Foot of Fore Mast
	Tackle	1	2"	9 7/8		B9	8"	2 Blocks	
122a	Hallyard	1	2"	23		B9	8"	1 Block	Forecastle
	Strapping		2"	1					
122b	Sheets	2	2½"	19 5/8		B9	9"	2 Blocks	Forecastle
	Strapping		2½"	1					
122c	Outhauler	1	1½"	11 7/8		B9	6"		
122d	Downhauler	1	1"	17⅓		B9	5"		Forecastle
	Strapping		1"	1					
	Fore Topgallant Yard & Sail								
123	Parral Ropes *	2	1½"	3				6" Parral	
124	Tie *	1	2½"	5 1/8					
	Halyard		1½"	9		B9	6"	2 Blocks	Foot of Fore Mast
	Strapping		2"	1					
125	Horses	2	2"	5					
126	Braces	2	1½"	73¾		B9	6"	4 Blocks	Fore Rail
	Strapping	2	1½"	3⅔					

Item & No	Name	Quantity	Circumference	Length (Fathoms)	Notes	Blocks/Hearts Type	Blocks/Hearts Size	Notes	Belays To
	Running Rigging								
127	Lifts	2	2"	37	Single	B9	6"	2 Blocks	Fore Top
	Strapping	2	2½"					2 Thimbles	
128	Sheets	2	1"	24⅔		B9	5"	2 Blocks	Fore Shrouds
	Strapping	2	1"	2		C	6"	2 Cleats	
129	Clue Lines	2	1"	47¼		B12	5"	2 Blocks.C,6",2	Fore Shrouds
	Strapping	2	1"	2		B9	5"	2 Blocks	
130	Bow Lines	2	1"	47¼		C	6",2	6 Thimbles	Forecastle
	Bridles	2	1"	6					
131	Spare								
132	Earrings *	2	¾"	18½					
133	Shifting Backstay	2	2½"	13½				1 Thimble	
*	Tackle	2	1½"	5¾		B9	6"	2 Blocks	
	Strapping		1½"	1					
	Fore Topgallant Studding Sail								
134	Halyards	2	1½"	42 7/8		B9	6"	6 Blocks	Fore Top
134a	Sheets	2	1"	21½		B9	6"	2 Blocks	Top Mast Shrouds
134b	Tacks	2	1½"	31½		B9	6"	2 Blocks	Fore Top
	Down Haulers *	2	1"	21½					Fore Top
	Strapping		1½"	6 1/8					
	Jib								
135	Jib Stay	1	3"	16 7/8		B9	9"	1 Block	Carrick Bitts
	Strapping		3"	1					
	Tackle Fall		1½"	12½		B9	6"	2 Blocks	
	Strapping		1½"	1					
136	Jib Halyard	1	2½"	24 3/8		B9	9"	1 Block	
	Strapping		2½"	1					
136a	Downhauler	1	1½"	22 1/8		B9	6"	1 Block	Forecastle
136b	Sheets		2½"	23 5/8	Single	C	8"	1 Cleat	Forecastle
	Main Yard & Sail								
137	Truss Pendant *	2	4½"	6 7/8		B10	8"	2 Blocks, 4 Thimbles	
	Falls	2	2"	25 5/8		B10	8"	2 Blocks	
	Strapping		2½"	2¼					Cleat on Mast
Truss Pendant	Eye Seizing	2	¾"	6 7/8					
	Nave Line	1	1"	8¼		B9	6"		Foot of Main Mast
138	Jeer Falls	2	2½"	55		B1	20"	3 Blocks	Foot of Main Mast
	Strapping		5",4",2½"	6 7/8		B10	12"	4 Blocks	
	Seizing		1"	13¾					
	Lashing, Masthead	2	7"	20 5/8					
Jeers	Lashing, Yard	2	3"	6 7/8					
	Tye	2	2"	11		B1	12"	2 Blocks	
139	Horses	2	3½"	6 7/8				2 Thimbles	
	Stirrups	6	2½"	6 7/8				6 Thimbles	
	Lanyards		1"	2¼					
140	Yard Tackle Pendant	2	4½"	4 1/8		B6	11"	2 Blocks	
	Falls	2	2½"	41		B5	9"	2 Blocks	Quarter Deck
	Strapping		3"	4 1/8					
141	Inner Tricing Line	2	1½"	17½		B6	6"	2 Blocks.C,8",2	Main Shrouds
142	Outer Tricing Line	2	1½"	17½		B6	6"	2 Blocks.C,8",2	Main Shrouds
	Strapping		1½"	3					
143	Braces	2	2½"	39 5/8		B9	9"	2 Blocks	Quarter Deck
	Pendants		3½"	4 1/8		B9	9"	2 Blocks	
	Preventer		2½"	5 1/8					
Braces	Strapping	2	2½"	1 3/8					
	Lashing		¾"	10¼					
144	Lifts	2	3"	51¼		B9	9"	4 Blocks	Quarter Deck
	Span for the Cap	1	4"	4 1/8		B13	14"	2 Blocks	
Lifts	Short Span		3"	1 3/8					
	Strapping		3"	2½					
145	Sheets	2	4½"	41	Cabled	B4	14"	2 Blocks	Quarter Deck
	Strapping		4½"			B9	14"	2 Blocks	
Sheets	Seizing		¾"	6 7/8					
	Stoppers	2	3	4					
146	Tacks	2	5½"	35 7/8	Taper & Cabled	B11	15"	2 Blocks	Waist
	Strapping		4"	4½					
	Seizing		¾"	7¼					
147	Clue Garnets	2	2½"	30¾		B12	9"	2 Blocks	
	Strap		2½"	3 7/8		B9	9"	2 Blocks	Main Rail
	Strapping		2½"	1					
148	Leechline Legs	2	2"	23½		B6	9"	2 Blocks	
	Falls	2	2"	23½		B9	9"	4 Blocks	Main Rail
	Strapping		2½"	5 7/8					
149	Buntline Legs	4	2"	23½		B10	8"	4 Blocks	
	Falls	4	2"	23½		B9	8"	8 Blocks	Fore Brace Bitts
	Strapping		2½"	5 7/8					
150	Slablines	2	1½"	15½		B9	6"	2 Blocks	Main Rail
	Strapping		1½"	2					

Running Rigging

Item & No	Name	Quantity	Circumference	Length (Fathoms)	Notes	Blocks/Hearts Type	Blocks/Hearts Size	Notes	Belays To
151	Bowlines	2	3"	24 5/8		B10	12"	1 Block	
	Bridles	4	3"	6				6 Thimbles	
	Strapping		3"	1 1/2					
	Seizing		3/4"	1 1/2					
	Lashing		1"	1 1/2					
Bowlines	Tackle		2"	6		B9	8"	2 Blocks	Foot of Fore Mast
	Strapping		2"	2		B10	8"	2 Blocks	
152	Earrings *	2	1 1/2"	13 2/3					
153	Quarter Tackle Pendant	2	4 1/2"	7		B10	11"	2 Blocks	
*	Falls	2	2 1/2"	35 7/8		B9	13"	2 Blocks	
	Strapping		3 1/2"	3 1/2		B9	11"	2 Blocks	
154	Luff Tackles *	3	2 1/2"	75		B9	10"	3 Blocks	
	Strapping		3"	6		B10	10"	3 Blocks	
	Main Lower Studding Sail								
155	Fore Guy	2	2"	30 5/8		B9	7"	2 Blocks	Fore Channel
	Strapping	2	2"	1					
156	After Guy	2	2"	25 1/2		B9	7"	2 Blocks	Mizzen Channel
	Strapping	2	2"	1					
157	Topping Lift *	2	2 1/2"	20 1/2		B9	8"	2 Blocks	Foot of Main Mast
	Span	1	3"	6 1/8					
158	Inner Halyard	2	2"	24 3/8		B9	9"	4 Blocks	Foot of Main Mast
159	Outer Halyard	2	2 1/2"	43		B9	9"	4 Blocks	Foot of Main Mast
160	Sheets	2	2"	12 3/8		B9	9"	2 Blocks	Mizzen Channel
161	Tacks	2	2 1/2"	22 3/4		B9	9"	2 Blocks	Fore Channel
	Strapping		2 1/2"	8 1/4					
	Main Stay Sail								
162	Staysail Stay	1	3"	7 7/8				2 Thimbles	Fore Mast
	Collar	1	3"	2					
	Seizing		3/4"	6					
	Lanyards		1"	4					
162a	Halyard	1	2"	22		B9	8"	3 Blocks	Foot of Main Mast
162b	Sheets	2	2"	7 7/8		B9	8"	2 Blocks	Waist
162c	Tacks		2"	2 5/8					Foremast
	Downhauler *	1	1 1/2"	11 7/8		B9	6"	1 Block	
	Strapping		1 1/2"	1					
	Main Top Yard & Sail								
163	Parral Ropes *	2	2"	6 1/4				14" Parral	
164	Tie	1	4"	27					Main Channel, St'bd
*	Strapping		4"	5 1/2	Served				
	Seizing		3/4"	10 7/8					
Tie	Lashers, Mast	2	1 1/2"	7 1/4	Served	B3	14"	1 Block	
	Lashers, Yard		1"	3 5/8	Served				
165	Horses	2	3"	6 1/4					
	Stirrups	4	2"	4 5/8				4 Thimbles	
166	Flemish Horses	2	3"						
167	Braces	2	2"	37 1/4		B9	8"	4 Blocks	Mizzen Topsail Bitts
	Pendants		3"	3 7/8		B9	8"	2 Blocks	
	Strapping	2	2"	1 1/2					
Braces	Preventers	2	2"	4 7/8					
	Span	1	3 1/2"	4	Around Mizzen Mast				
168	Lifts	2	2 1/2"	34 7/8		B14	14"	2 Blocks, with 169	Main Shrouds
Lifts	Beckets	2	2 1/2"	2		C	10"	2 Cleats	
	Strapping		2 1/2"	6		B9	8"	4 Blocks	
169	Reef Tackle Pend'ts	2	2 1/2"	23 1/4		B9	7"	2 Blocks	
	Falls	2	1 1/2"	31		B14	14"	2 Blocks, with 168	Top Mast Shrouds
	Strapping		2"	1 1/2					
170	Sheets	2	4 1/2"	27 1/8		B4	14"	2 Blocks	Fore Brace Bitts
	Straps, Blocks	2	5"	2 3/4		B11	14"	2 Blocks	
	Straps, quarter Blocks	2	4"	4 1/8		B9	14"	2 Blocks	
	Lashers, quarter Blocks	2	1"	5 1/2					
	Seizing	2	3/4"	10 1/8					
Sheets	Span		3"	4 1/2					
	Stoppers	2	3"	2 1/4					
171	Clue Lines	2	2"	46 1/2		B12	8"	2 Blocks C, 10", 2	Main Shrouds
	Strapping		2"	4 5/8		B9	8"	2 Blocks	
172	Bunt Lines	2	2"	35		B9	7"	2 Blocks C, 10", 2	Main Shrouds
	Strapping		2"	2		B9	7"	2 Blocks	
173	Leech Lines	2	1 1/2"	14 1/2		B9	6	2 Blocks	Main Rail
	Strapping		1 1/2"	1					
174	Bow Lines	2	2 1/2"	30		B9	9"	2 Blocks	Foot of Fore Mast
	Bridles	4	2 1/2"	7 3/4				6 Thimbles	
Bow Lines	Strapping		2 1/2"	1					
	Lashing		3/4"	6 1/4					
175	Halyards	2	2 1/2"	72		B10	14"	2 Blocks	Quarter Deck
	Strapping		3 1/2"	4 1/2		B9	14"	2 Blocks	
	Seizing		3/4"	9					
176	Slings *	1	3 1/2"	6 1/4					
177	Earring *	2	1"	20 2/3					

Running Rigging

Item & No	Name	Quantity	Circumference	Length (Fathoms)	Notes	Blocks/Hearts Type	Blocks/Hearts Size	Notes	Belays To
	Main Top Studding Sail								
178	Halyards	2	2"	46 1/2		B9	8"	6 Blocks	Main Top
179	Sheets	2	1 1/2"	32 1/4		B9	8"	2 Blocks	Foot of Main Mast
180	Tacks	2	2"	31		B9	8"	2 Blocks	Main Channel
181	Downhauler *	2	1"	28		B9	6"	2 Blocks	Main Channel
182	Tails		2"	9 7/8					
183	Straps		2"	3 1/8					
	Main Top Stay Sail								
184	Halyards	1	2 1/2"	27 1/2		B9	8"	1 Block	Main Rail, Port
	Strapping		2 1/2"	1					
184a	Sheets	2	2 1/2"	42 3/4		B9	8"	2 Blocks	Waist
	Strapping		2 1/2"	4					
184b	Tack		2"	3					Fore Shrouds
184c	Down Hauler	1	1 1/2"	16 1/2		B9	6"	2 Blocks	
	Strapping		1 1/2"	1					
	Main Topgallant Yard & Sail								
185	Parral Ropes *	2	1 1/2"	3				7" Parral	
186	Tie	1	2 1/2"	10 7/8		B9	6"	2 Blocks	Foot of Main Mast
	Halyard		1 1/2"	21 5/8					
	Strapping		2"	1 1/2					
187	Horses	2	2"	5					
188	Braces	2	1 1/2"	43		B9	6"	4 Blocks	Mizzen Shrouds
	Strapping	2	1 1/2"	2		C	8"	2 Cleats	
189	Lifts	2	2"	37	Single	B9	6"	2 Blocks	Main Top
	Strapping	2	2 1/2"					2 Thimbles	
190	Sheets	2	1"	31		B9	5"	2 Blocks	Main Shrouds
	Strapping	2	1"	2		C	6"	2 Cleats	
191	Clue Lines	2	1"	49 1/4		B12	5"	2 Blocks. C, 6", 2	Main Shrouds
	Strapping	2	1"			B9	5"	2 Blocks	
192	Bow Lines	2	1"	49 1/4		C	6"	2 Cleats	Carrick Bitts
	Bridles	2	1"					2 Thimbles	
193	Spare								
194	Earrings *	2	3/4"	18 1/2					
195	Shifting Back Stay	2	2 1/2"	14 1/4				1 Thimble	
*	Tackle	2	1"	14		B9	5"	2 Blocks	
	Strapping		1"	1 1/2					
	Main Topgallant Studding Sail								
196	Halyards	2	1 1/2"	45		B9	6"	6 Blocks	Main Top
196a	Sheets	2	1"	22 1/2		B9	6"	2 Blocks	Top Mast Shrouds
196b	Tacks	2	1 1/2"	32 1/2		B9	6"	2 Blocks	Main Top
	Downhaulers *	2	1	22 1/2					Main Top
	Strapping		1 1/2	6 1/8					
	Main Top Gallant Stay Sail								
197	Stay	1	2"	24 1/2		B9	7"	1 Block	Fore Top
197a	Halyard	1	1 1/2"	34 1/2		B9	6"	1 Block	Waist
197b	Sheets	2	1 1/2"	34 1/2		B9	6"	2 Blocks	Waist
197c	Tack		1"	6					Main Top
197d	Downhauler	1	1"	21 1/2		B9	5"	2 Blocks	
	Strapping		1 1/2	2					
	Cross Jack Yard								
198	Span about the Cap *	1	2"	1					
199	Slings	1 pr	3"	3				1 Thimble	
	Strapping		2 1/2"	1 1/2					
200	Braces	2	1 1/2"	32 1/2		B9	6"	2 Blocks	Main Rail
	Pendants		2"	5		B9	6"	2 Blocks	
	Strapping		2"	2					
201	Lifts	2	1 1/2"	26 1/8	Running	B9	6"	4 Blocks	Mizzen Sheet Bitts
	Strapping		1 1/2"	2					
	Mizzen Stay Sail								
202	Stay	1	3"	8				2 Thimbles	Foot of Main Mast
	Collar	1	2 1/2"	2				1 Thimble	
	Lanyard		1"	4					
202a	Halyard		2"	16		B9	7"	3 Blocks	
202b	Sheets	2	2"	8		B9	7"	1 Block	Foot of Mizzen Mast
202c	Tack		2"	2					Foot of Main Mast
202d	Downhauler		1"	8		B9	5"	1 Block	
	Strapping		1 1/2"	2					
	Mizzen Top Yard & Sail								
203	Parral Ropes *	2	1 1/2"	3				8" Parral	
204	Tie	1	3"	8					Mizzen Sheet Bitts
	Halyard		2"	24 1/4		B9	8"	2 Blocks	
	Strapping		2 1/2"	2					
205	Horses	2	2"	4 7/8					
206	Braces	2	1 1/2"	33		B9	6"	4 Blocks	Cleat on Taffrail
	Pendants		1 1/2"	3		C	6"	2 Cleats	
207	Lifts	2	2"	34	Single			2 Thimbles	Aft Rail
208	Sheets	2	3"	21		B11	10"	2 Blocks	Mizzen Sheet Bitts
	Strapping		3"	2, 2		B9	10"	2 Blocks	
	Lashing		3/4"	4					

H Rigging

Running Rigging

Item & No	Name	Quantity	Circumference	Length (Fathoms)	Notes	Blocks/Hearts Type	Blocks/Hearts Size	Notes	Belays To
209	Clue Lines	2	1½"	36		B12	5"	2 Blocks	Aft Rail
	Strapping		1½"			B9	5"	2 Blocks	
210	Bunt Lines	2	1½"	26		B9	6"	4 Blocks	Aft Rail
	Strapping		1½"					1 Thimble	
211	Bowlines	2	1½"	23		B9	5"	2 Blocks	Main Rail
	Bridles	4	1½"	4⅞				4 Thimbles	
	Strapping		1½"	1					
	Mizzen Top Stay Sail								
212	Halyard	1	1½"	14½		B9	6"	1 Block	Foot of Mizzen Mast
212a	Sheets	2	1½"	16½		B9	6"	2 Blocks	Aft Rail
212b	Tack	2	1½"	2					
212c	Downhauler	1	1"	10⅛		B9	5"	1 Block	
	Mizzen Course & Driver Gaff								
213	Parral Ropes *							Trucks only	
214	Derrick	1	2½"	24		B10	10"	1 Block	Quarter Deck
Derrick	Span	1	2½"	3		B9	9"	1 Block	
	Strapping		3"	2					
	Lashing		1"	7					
215	Peak Halyard	1	1"	12		B9	5"	1 Block	Quarter Deck
216	Vang Pendants	2	3"	6⅞					
	Falls	2	1½"	20½		B9	6"	4 Blocks	Taffrail
	Strapping		1½"	1		C	6"	2 Cleats	
217	Earring *	1	¾"	8					
218	Lacing, Mast		2"	12					
219	Lacing, Yard		¾"	19					
220	Brail Peak Legs		1½"	10					
	Falls		1½"	16		B9	6"	4 Blocks	
220a	Throat	1pr.	2"	15		B9	7"	2 Blocks	Foot of Mizzen Mast
220b	Middle	1pr.	1½	12		B9	6"	2 Blocks	Mizzen Shrouds
220c	Foot	1pr.	1½"	21		B9	6"	2 Blocks	After Rail
	Strapping		2"	7				4 Thimbles	
221	Sheet	1	2½"	16		B9	9"	2 Blocks	Quarter Deck
	Strapping		2½"	2					
222	Tack		1½"	3					Quarter Deck

* Not Shown on Drawings

Necessary Ropes

Item & No	Name	Quantity	Circumference	Length (Fathoms)	Notes	Blocks/Hearts Type	Blocks/Hearts Size	Notes
	Ground Tackle							
223	Cables *	6	12"	600	Cabled			
224	Stream Cable *	1	7"	100	Cabled			
225	Cat Falls	2	3"			B10	14"	2 Blocks
*	Lanyards		2"					
	Stoppers		2"					
226	Masthead Guy		5"					
*	Fore Guy		5"					
	Aft Guy		3"					
227	Pendants *	1	5½"			B9	15"	1 Block
Fish Tackle	Fall	1	3"			B13	24"	1 Block
	Strapping		3½"			B9	14"	1 Block
	Seizing		¾"					
	Lanyard		1½"					
228	Anchor Stock Tack	1	2"			B9	8"	1 Block
*	Anchor Stock Fall	1	2"			B10	8"	1 Block
229	Bill Pendants		2"					
*	Strapping		2½"					
230	Bower Anchor	2	5"					
*	Sheet Anchor	1	5"					
	Stream Anchor	1	3"					
	Kedge Anchor	1	2½"					
	Seizing		¾"					
	Wing		5"		Cabled			
	Dog		5"					
Stoppers	Seizing		¾"					
	Deck & Bitt		7"		Cabled			10 Thimbles
	Lanyards		2"					
	Seizing		1"					
231	Bower Anchor		4"		Cabled			
*	Sheet Anchor		4"		Cabled			
Buoy Ropes	Stream Anchor		3"		Cabled			
	Kedge Anchor		2½"		Cabled			
	Steering Gear							
232	Tiller Ropes		3"			B9	10"	8 Blocks
	Strapping		3"					
233	Rudder Pendants *		4"		Cabled			4 Thimbles
	Halyards							
234	Ensign Staff *		¾"					
235	Jack Staff *		¾"					
236	Pendant Slings *		¾"					
	Four Pounder Guns							
237	Breeching Rope *	4						
238	Side Tackle *	4pr	B9			B9, B10		8 of each Block
239	Train Tackle *	4	B9, B10			B9, B10		4 of each Block
	Rigging for Cutter & Launch							
240	Burton Pendants		3"			B9	8"	2 Blocks
	Runner		2½"					2 Thimbles
	Falls		2½"			B10	8"	2 Blocks
	Strapping		2"			B9	8"	2 Blocks
241	Shrouds	4	3"					4 Thimbles
	Lanyard		1"					
242	Stay	1	3½"					1 Thimble
	Lanyard		1"					
243	Main Halyard		1½"			B9	6"	1 Block
244	Outer Halyard		1½"			B9	6"	1 Block
	Sheet		1½"		B10, 5", 1 Block /	B9	5"	1 Block
	Downhauler		1"			B9	5"	1 Block, 2 Thimbles
	Strapping		1½"					
	Topping Lift		1½"					
245	Fore Halyard		1½"					
	Sheet		1½"					
	Tack		1"					
	Bowline		1½"					
246	Jib Halyard		1½"					
	Sheet		1½"					
	Out Hauler		1½"					
	In Hauler		¾"					
247	Boat Rope		4½"		Cabled			
	Lanyard		2"					
248	Guest Rope Cable		3"					
249	Grapnel Rope		3½"		Cabled			1 Thimble
250	Painter		3½"					1 Thimble
251	Stern Fast		2"					1 Thimble
252	Fenders		4"		Cabled			
	Lanyards		1½					
253	Rudder Lanyards		1"					
254	Crowfeet		¾"		13" Euphroe - Fore	B9	6"	2 Blocks
					23" Euphroe - Main	B9	8"	2 Blocks
					11" Euphroe - Mizzen	B9	5"	2 Blocks

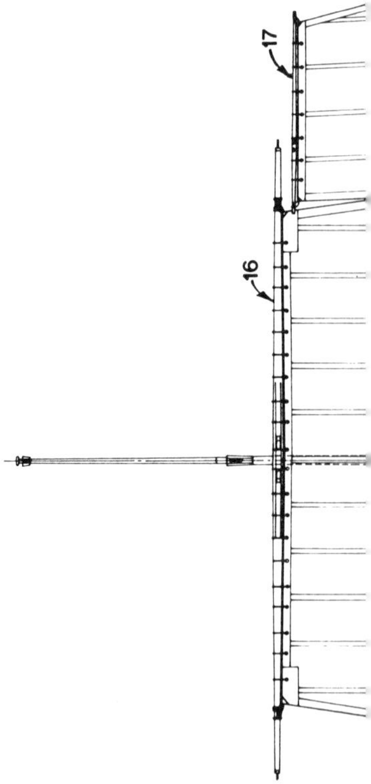

I Sails

I1/1   Foremast sails (1/96 scale)

1. Fore course
2. Fore topsail
3. Fore topgallant sail
4. Fore studding sail
5. Fore top studding sail
6. Fore topgallant studding sail
7. Forecastle
8. Foremast
9. Fore lower studding sail boom
10. Fore yard
11. Fore top studding sail boom
12. Fore studding sail yard
13. Fore top yard
14. Fore topgallant studding sail boom
15. Fore top studding sail yard
16. Fore topgallant yard
17. Fore topgallant studding sail yard

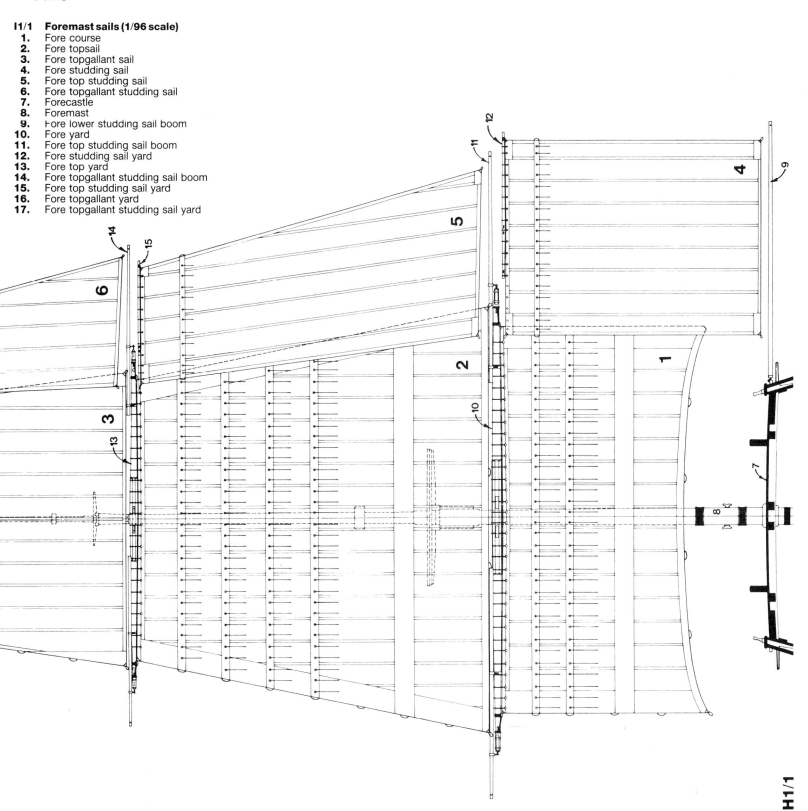

H1/1

I Sails

I2/1 Mainmast sails (1/96 scale)
  1. Main course
  2. Main topsail
  3. Main topgallant sail
  4. Main studding sail
  5. Main top studding sail
  6. Main topgallant studding sail
  7. Upper deck
  8. Mainmast
  9. Main lower studding sail boom
 10. Main yard
 11. Main top studding sail boom
 12. Main studding sail yard
 13. Main top yard
 14. Main topgallant studding sail boom
 15. Main top studding sail yard
 16. Main topgallant yard
 17. Main topgallant studding sail yard

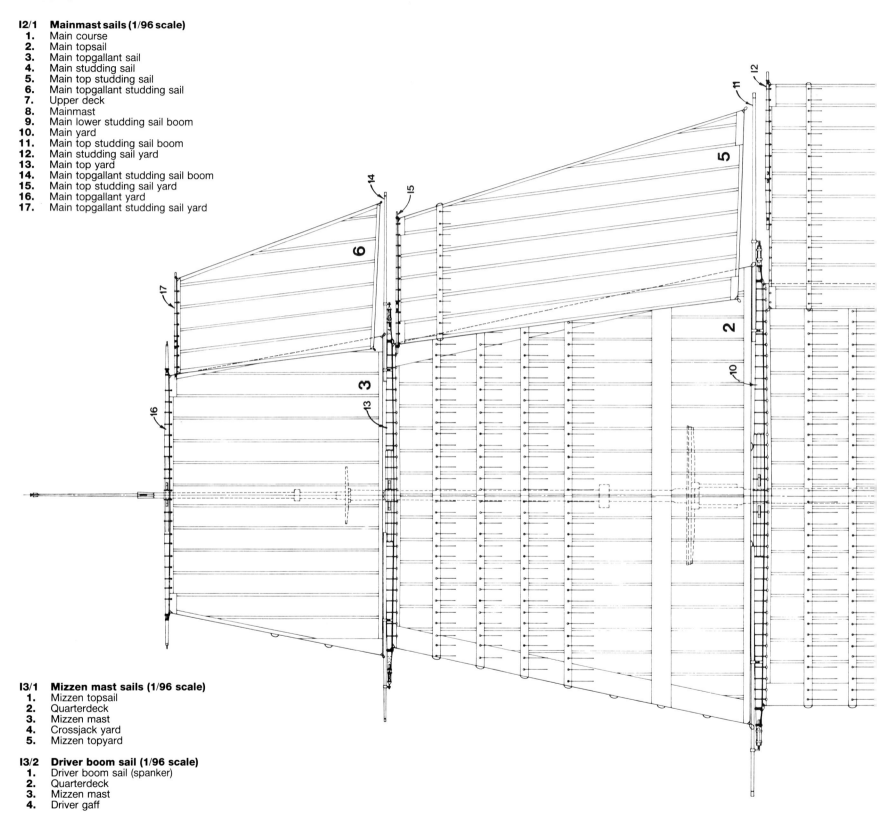

I3/1 Mizzen mast sails (1/96 scale)
  1. Mizzen topsail
  2. Quarterdeck
  3. Mizzen mast
  4. Crossjack yard
  5. Mizzen topyard

I3/2 Driver boom sail (1/96 scale)
  1. Driver boom sail (spanker)
  2. Quarterdeck
  3. Mizzen mast
  4. Driver gaff

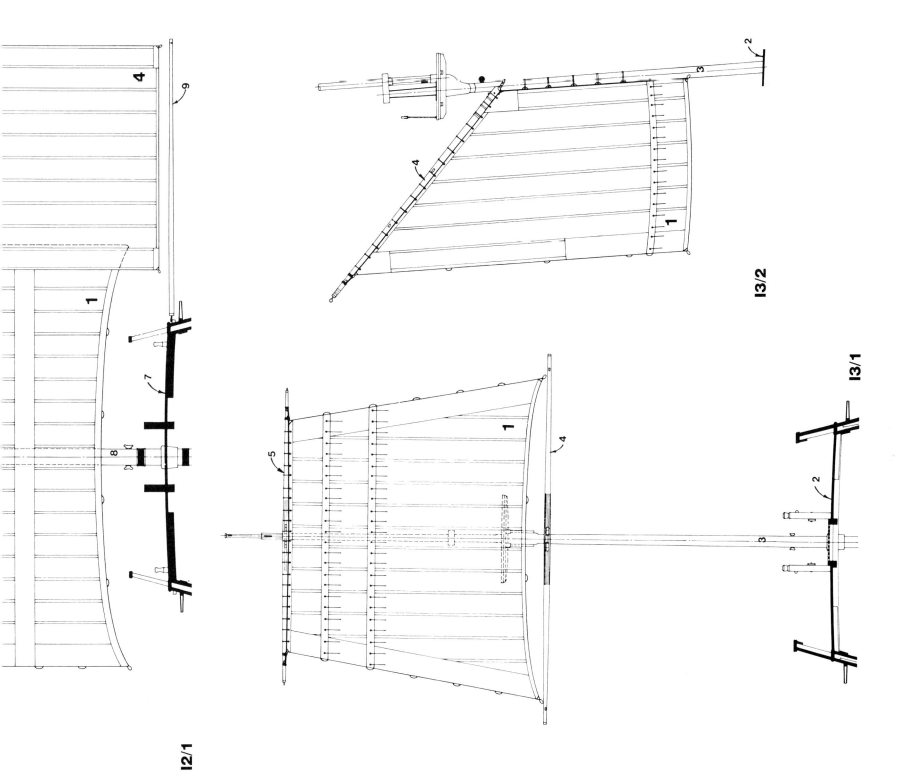

12/1

13/2

13/1

I Sails

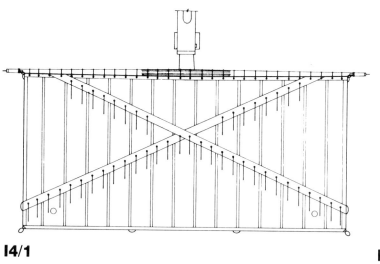

I4/1

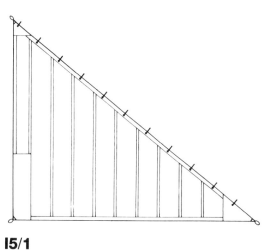

I5/1

I4/1   Spritsail (1/96 scale)

I4/2   Jib (1/96 scale)

I5/1   Fore staysail (1/96 scale)

I5/2   Fore topmast staysail (1/96 scale)

I5/3   Main staysail (1/96 scale)

I5/4   Main topmast staysail (1/96 scale)

I5/5   Main topgallant staysail
       (1/96 scale)

I5/6   Mizzen staysail (1/96 scale)

I5/7   Mizzen topmast staysail
       (1/96 scale)

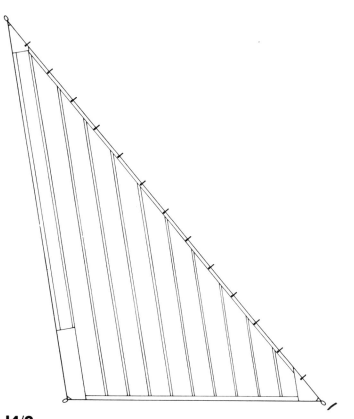

I4/2

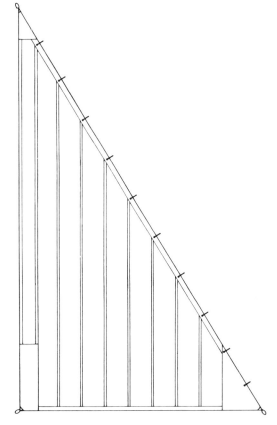

I5/2

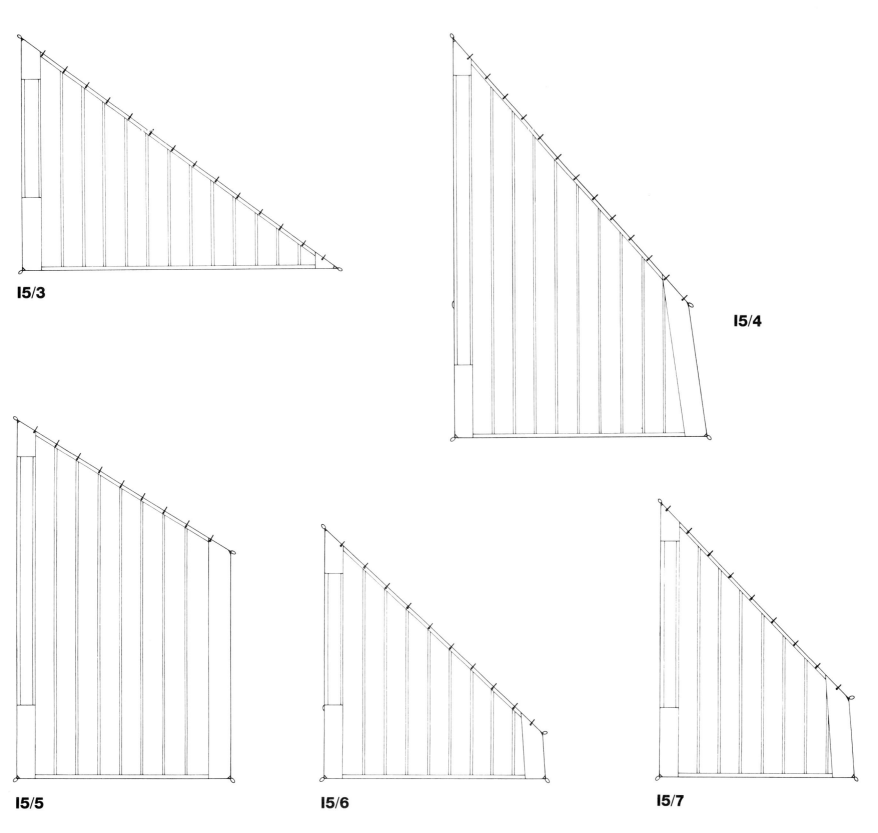

I5/3

I5/4

I5/5

I5/6

I5/7

117

I Sails

I5/8 **Staysails (1/192 scale)**
1. Fore staysail
2. Fore top staysail
3. Jibsail
4. Main staysail
5. Main top staysail
6. Main topgallant staysail
7. Mizzen staysail
8. Mizzen top staysail
9. Mizzen course (spanker)

I5/8

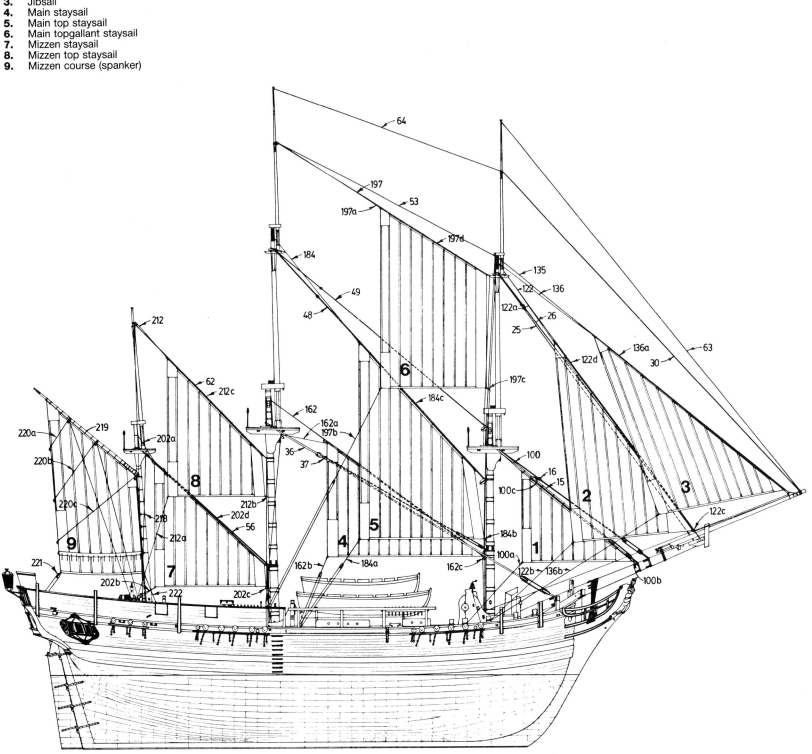

J Boats

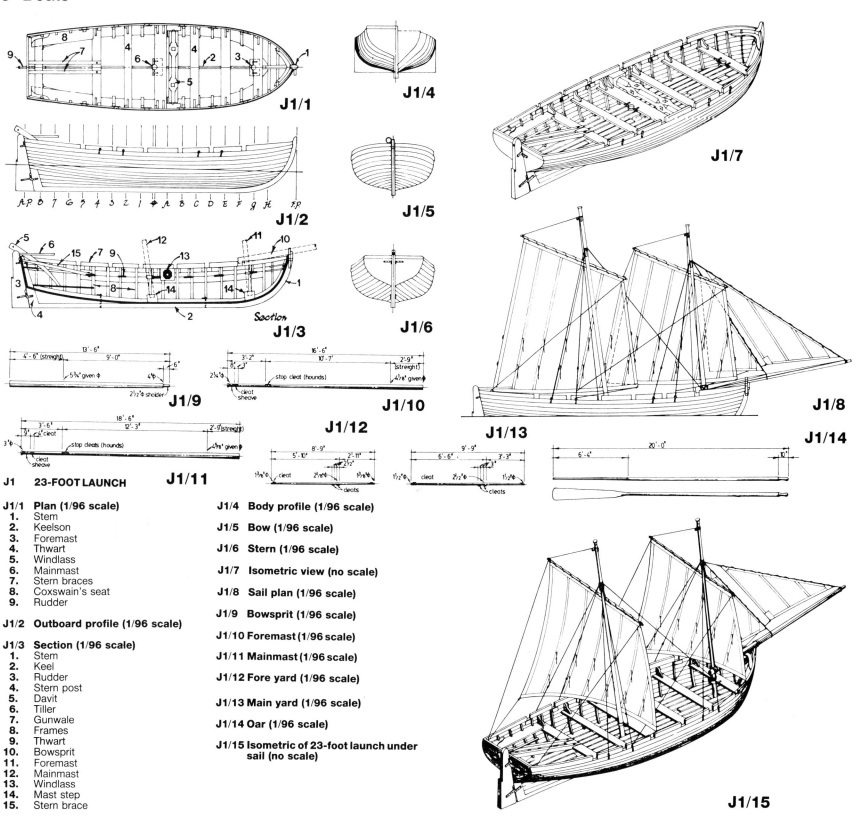

J1/1

J1/4

J1/2

J1/5

J1/3

Section

J1/6

J1/7

J1/8

J1/9

J1/10

J1/12

J1/13

J1/14

J1/11

J1/15

J1   23-FOOT LAUNCH

J1/1   Plan (1/96 scale)
1. Stem
2. Keelson
3. Foremast
4. Thwart
5. Windlass
6. Mainmast
7. Stern braces
8. Coxswain's seat
9. Rudder

J1/2   Outboard profile (1/96 scale)

J1/3   Section (1/96 scale)
1. Stem
2. Keel
3. Rudder
4. Stern post
5. Davit
6. Tiller
7. Gunwale
8. Frames
9. Thwart
10. Bowsprit
11. Foremast
12. Mainmast
13. Windlass
14. Mast step
15. Stern brace

J1/4   Body profile (1/96 scale)

J1/5   Bow (1/96 scale)

J1/6   Stern (1/96 scale)

J1/7   Isometric view (no scale)

J1/8   Sail plan (1/96 scale)

J1/9   Bowsprit (1/96 scale)

J1/10   Foremast (1/96 scale)

J1/11   Mainmast (1/96 scale)

J1/12   Fore yard (1/96 scale)

J1/13   Main yard (1/96 scale)

J1/14   Oar (1/96 scale)

**J1/15   Isometric of 23-foot launch under
          sail (no scale)**

J Boats

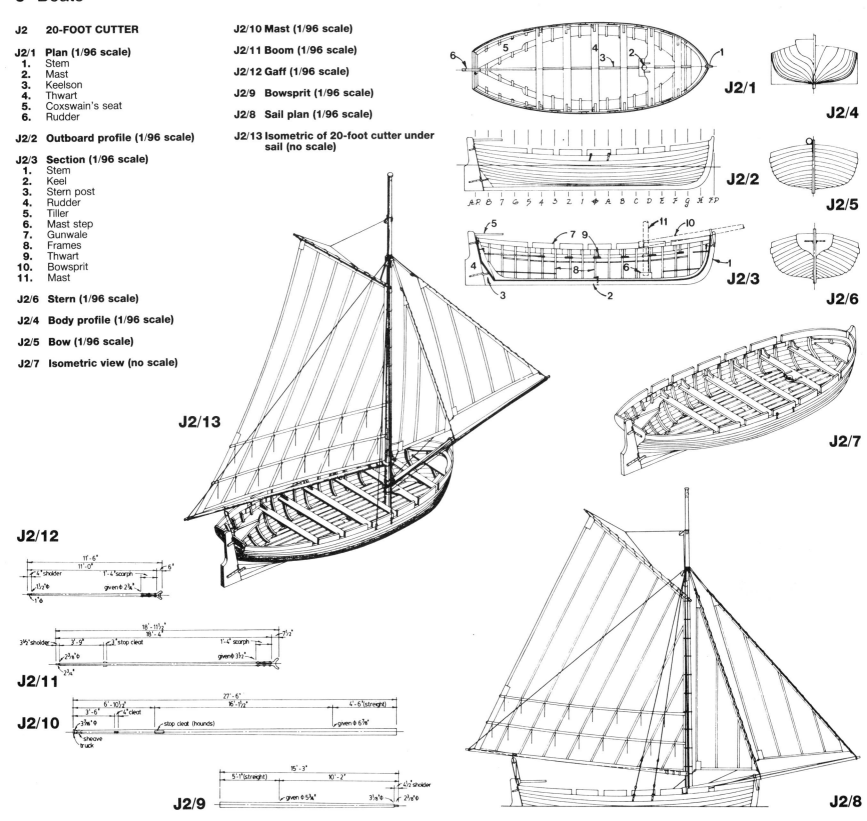

J2   20-FOOT CUTTER

J2/1   Plan (1/96 scale)
1. Stem
2. Mast
3. Keelson
4. Thwart
5. Coxswain's seat
6. Rudder

J2/2   Outboard profile (1/96 scale)

J2/3   Section (1/96 scale)
1. Stem
2. Keel
3. Stern post
4. Rudder
5. Tiller
6. Mast step
7. Gunwale
8. Frames
9. Thwart
10. Bowsprit
11. Mast

J2/6   Stern (1/96 scale)

J2/4   Body profile (1/96 scale)

J2/5   Bow (1/96 scale)

J2/7   Isometric view (no scale)

J2/10 Mast (1/96 scale)

J2/11 Boom (1/96 scale)

J2/12 Gaff (1/96 scale)

J2/9   Bowsprit (1/96 scale)

J2/8   Sail plan (1/96 scale)

**J2/13 Isometric of 20-foot cutter under
        sail (no scale)**

J2/1

J2/4

J2/2

J2/5

J2/3

J2/6

J2/7

J2/13

J2/12

J2/11

J2/10

J2/9

J2/8